Dear John —

I hope we
can do a
book together
soon.

Sincerely,

McCaffry

Thomas

REVISED EDITION

IN-HOUSE TELEMARKETING

THE

MASTERPLAN

FOR STARTING

AND MANAGING

A PROFITABLE

TELEMARKETING

PROGRAM

Thomas A.
McCAFFERTY

PROBUS PUBLISHING COMPANY
Chicago, Illinois
Cambridge, England

ISBN 1-55738-529-7

Printed in the United States of America

BB

1 2 3 4 5 6 7 8 9 0

Contents

Preface:
Getting an Edge
on the Competition

From now until the turn of the century, you'll experience more market-making, market-breaking changes than in any previous decade in history. Changes are occurring on all levels—technological, political, social. Telemarketing isn't a panacea, but it sure can help.

The long-awaited promises of computer technology are about to affect marketing, as they have manufacturing and MIS (management information systems) over the last decade. I remember reading Alvin Toffler's *Future Shock* and John Naisbitt's *Megatrends* when they were first published. They forecast computerized manufacturing facilities producing customized products on a mass scale: everything would be made to order. This is finally beginning to happen. Additionally, computer technology has made just-in-time inventory control possible and has substantially improved quality control.

Back in the 1960s and 1970s, workers' fears of computers taking over their jobs were groundless. Every time a company installed a mainframe, more people were hired, and more paper was generated and shuffled. Now, however, MISs are on the verge of actually generating paperless transactions on a large scale in several key industries; the fear of white-collar job losses is finally justified. Currently, we're seeing this specifically in the defense industry—and on the middle-management level of just about all industries in general.

What's the point of having a supplier who can deliver components within 24 hours if your purchase order takes five days to be delivered by the post office? Electronic mail can deliver it in seconds. Or a fax (facsimile transmission) provides a hard copy in minutes.

This is called EDI, or electronic data interchange, and it is the first step in total "electronic commerce." The next step is electronic data integration, by which electronically transmitted purchase orders, for example, automatically enter vendors' systems. The POs immediately notify inventory control and alert the manufacturing departments or prepare pick-tickets for a warehousemen. In some sophisticated operations, packing slips, shipping arrangements, and invoices are automatically generated. A debit now can be automatically transmitted to the buyer's bank for approval and payment. The jobs of scores of bean counters and paper shufflers are in jeopardy.

It may have taken 30 years for the promise of the computer to be fulfilled, but it is finally upon us. There is even a bonus for some. As always, those companies that took the lead have a competitive edge. To understand this statement, all you need to do is look at what the Japanese did to our automobile and electronic markets.

Some retailers are making the most of this technology. For example, some distributors of gasoline have learned to use electronic data interchange to their advantage. A customer drives up to a pump and inserts a credit or debit card into a card reader, which performs a quick credit check and activates it. The pump is on a computer network that may be hundreds of miles away. When the customer replaces the nozzle, the transaction is automatically terminated and a receipt is printed.

More customers can be handled using this method, and more gas pumped. Costs are lower. Customers appreciate not having to walk to a cashier in inclement weather and wait to pay. The oil company gathers more information about its customers and their driving patterns to use in future merchandising efforts, often telemarketing. On top of all this, retailers have found that this service is so convenient, they have built loyalty among their customers—something that has always been lacking among gas credit card holders.

This isn't a futuristic story. Eighty percent of Mobil Oil Company's 10,000 U.S. stations are on POS (point of sale) computer networks—and they are expanding into dozens of foreign countries. Some of the 24-hour stations, online with the main computer, do not have to be manned around the clock. Other savings occur due to less fraud and fewer robberies, since little cash is onsite.

What does all this have to do with telemarketing? Plenty, because computer technology is now overwhelming the way you market. You'll need to think automation to be competitive. This all becomes even more meaningful when you study the demographics of the U.S. marketplace. It is forcing you to provide better service at a lower price, to pay closer attention to current customers, and to look for new opportunities. You simply have to become more competitive. Telemarketing offers several solutions, but first let's quickly analyze the situation.

David Birch, president of Cognetica, has a handle on what's happening, in my opinion. His reputation was made a decade ago when his work uncovered the fact that job growth in the 1980s would come from small companies. Birch analyzed the 20 million jobs generated and learned that during that decade, the *Fortune* 500 corporations *cut* employment by 4 million. The conclusion: small companies created 25 million jobs!

This was a very important insight. It made us aware that the service sector was the area of growth. The Baby Boomers and women flowed into this job vacuum. The economy fed on itself.

The Baby Boomers—this enormous group of consumers born just after World War II—were the engine that drove the economy for the last two decades. Think of the economy as a boa constrictor that has swallowed a piglet. As the snake digests its dinner, you can see it move slowly through its body. Eventually, it is gone.

It's Birch's contention that the economy has digested the Baby Boomers. They have bought the home of their dreams, put their kids through college, bought just about all the cars they need, all the furniture, all the major appliances, etc., etc. Now they want to plan for retirement . . . consolidate, save some money, or pay off debts.

The key statistic, in Birch's opinion, is the birth rate. It has been declining in this country over the last century, with the exception of the Baby Boomers. Now it's back on track—downward. From this decline in population, all else flows.

Back in the 1980s, when the *Fortune* 500 were laying off 4 million employees, many took their severance pay and started small manufacturing plants. They hired 10, 50, 100 or more people. Or they created new service organizations, generating jobs.

This phenomenon isn't happening today. The market just isn't there to absorb additional production. Laid-off middle managers now become investment bankers or consultants; few new ancillary positions result, because the computer has so automated the modern office. Many can find only part-time or temporary work. In other words, small businesses won't fuel the economy, according to Birch.

What he sees is a 1 percent annual growth rate as the norm for the next decade or two. Just as automation helped manufacturing to become more efficient by replacing people with robots in the 1980s, technology is streamlining service and clerical functions today. Computers, facsimile machines, hand-held computers, cellular phones, scanners, form readers, voice mail, and electronic forms are thinning the ranks of the secretaries and administrative assistants.

While the domestic marketplace refuses to expand at a rapid pace, the international market offers some unique opportunities. For example, the European Economic Community may offer one gigantic market once all the agreements and treaties are signed. The dissolution of the Union of Soviet Socialist Republics will eventually create markets only previously dreamed of by even the most optimistic telemarketer. The same is true for the Pacific Rim countries.

My point in all this political, technological, and sociological discussion is that you must change your thinking to be successful in the years ahead. To combat competition in a slow-growing economy requires a better price, more service, and new markets. This book will show you how telemarketing, both domestic and international, can help you sell in previously unreachable markets.

To get the most from your telemarketing, you'll also need to automate it, which we'll discuss later. I believe we are finally entering what Marshall McLuhan once described as the "global village," where we are all linked together by "hot" (fast-moving, electronic) media.

A giant step forward was taken by Bellcore, the lab of the seven Bell companies. It has developed a compression technology for digital signals so they can be transmitted over regular copper wire to any home or business with a digital telephone. Prior to this advancement, it was believed the next major step to reach consumers would have to wait until homes were wired with fiber-optic cable.

Simultaneously, President Clinton announced plans for "information superhighways" criss-crossing the country. Schools, hospitals, libraries, businesses—all linked by a nationwide computer network. The possibilities for the astute marketer (telemarketer) are mind-boggling.

One of the most effective marketing tools you'll want to use to take advantage of all these opportunities, and one that telemarketing is particularly suited for, is database marketing. While this concept may be new to some, it is what telemarketing sales representatives (TSRs) have been doing for the last two decades. Database marketing simply means building a detailed file of information on individual clients so you can better serve their needs. Who can do it more successfully than someone who talks regularly with each account? We'll spend a lot of time in this book discussing the market edge you can get with database telemarketing.

As with any skill, you need to learn the basics first. Then, when you have a firm foundation, you can refine and automate. Telemarketing is no different. This book has been written to give you a thorough understanding of the subject and to show you what additional steps you need to take to create a successful telemarketing operation for your business.

The only cloud in the blue sky is legislation.

At this point, you need to distinguish between business-to-business and consumer-targeted telemarketing. Business-to-business telemarketing will remain relatively free of legislation, while consumer telemarketing will be plagued by it. For this reason, smart telemarketing retailers are turning more and more to inbound, as opposed to outbound, telemarketing. This is a strong trend, and I expect it to continue. Therefore, I have substantially expanded the chapter on this subject in this revised edition.

As a professional, you'll need to be well aware of all the provisions of the Telephone Consumer Protection Act (TCPA). It went into effect on December 20, 1992, and instructs the Federal Communication Commission (FCC) to develop regulations to protect the privacy rights of residential telephone subscribers and to provide them a way of stopping unwanted calls. The FCC defines telephone sales as the "initiation of a telephone call or message for the purposes of encouraging the purchase or rental of, or investment in, property, goods or services, as is transmitted to any person." This very broad definition covers just about any telemarketing operation.

The following are key provisions of the FCC regulations:

- Telephone solicitation calls may not be made to residences before 8:00 a.m. or after 9:00 p.m., based on local time of the recipient.

- Companies making calls must maintain a list of people who do not wish to be called at all. This list must include their telephone number.

- TSRs are obligated to identify to the consumer the name of the company they are working for and to give them a phone number at which it can be contacted. In the case of service bureaus, the TSRs must identify the company on whose behalf the call is being made.

- The names of any persons requesting to be removed from a list must be shared between branches, departments, or divisions.

- A company is considered to be in compliance with the TCPA as long as someone requesting to be removed from a list is not called again.

- TCPA gives the consumer the right to bring suit against a violating company in his state's courts for up to $500 or actual monetary damages, whichever is greater. The consumer can also ask the FCC to pursue violators and the state's attorney general can take action.

- Unsolicited fax solicitations are also excluded by TCPA.

Since laws in this country are modified by each case that goes to trial, the rules and regulations will change. Therefore, it is impossible to provide up-to-date information in a book. You can keep on top of the law by reading industry publications, such as *DM News*, *Teleprofessional* and *TeleMarketing* magazines. A sample TCPA company policy can be found in the appendix.

Now, on to business!

What Is Telemarketing?

Telemarketing is the planned use of the telephone as a selling medium in conjunction with traditional marketing techniques to increase sales, reduce costs, and improve net income. The key terms are "planned" and "in conjunction with."

We all use the phone as a sales tool. The difference between unstructured use of the phone in selling and telemarketing is that in telemarketing, the phone actually becomes the sales medium. As such, it can be as effective as direct mail or person-to-person sales. For certain marketing tasks, it can be even more useful than the traditional approaches.

A successful telemarketing program is one that justifies its existence with positive bottom line performance. It requires responsible management and its own sales goals and budget. Most important, you must treat it as an independent profit center.

Telemarketing can be inbound or outbound. Inbound simply means the customer initiates calls, usually using a toll-free 800 number. In outbound telemarketing, the company calls the customer or prospect.

What Telemarketing Can Do

Below is a checklist of some of the things telemarketing does well. Consider where these activities fit into your marketing effort:

Direct selling
Seasonal selling
Special promotions
Setting appointments for your field sales force
Reactivating dormant accounts
Account management
Opening new sales territories
Cleaning prospect lists
Developing prospect lists
Qualifying prospects
Generating new leads
Backing up your field sales force
Creating awareness among customers, prospects and
      third-party influencers
Collecting overdue accounts
Market research
Defining markets
Test marketing
Positioning and pricing products
Product development
Fine-tuning marketing strategies
Learning about competition
Maintaining customer/shareholder relations
Overcoming negative publicity
Explaining unusual developments (name change, merger,
      sale of company)

Order taking
Solving service and parts problems
Cross-selling/upgrading
Renewing subscriptions
Updating records (taking changes of address)
Supplying information in response to inquiries
Qualifying/screening inquiries
Taking reservations (seminars, entertainment)
Tracking advertising/promotion/publicity

Following are some real-life examples of how telemarketing is currently used by some imaginative firms.

FINGERHUT

The telemarketing department began with the mission of verifying customer orders. The company quickly realized that once it had the customer on the line, an opportunity existed to sell additional merchandise. The company now has 120 sales reps who attempt to make 25,000 incremental sales a year.

GENERAL ELECTRIC

GE provides toll-free numbers to its customers. Its service department handles millions of calls a year. To find out how effective this service is, the company often surveys some of the people who call in. Of all customers questioned, 95 percent are satisfied with the way the calls are handled and the way their problems are resolved. GE believes that a satisfied customer will share his or her positive experience with the company with at least five friends. On the other hand, it is estimated that if a customer is unhappy with a product, 9 or 10 people will hear about it. As a result, GE receives millions of positive word-of-mouth recommendations each year from its telemarketing after-sales support.

3M

3M offers a toll-free service line for customer equipment problems. Thirty percent of all incoming service calls are taken care of within a few minutes, thereby saving the company the expense of sending a service technician to handle simple problems. 3M thus saves a significant amount of service costs and equipment downtime.

CLAIROL

Before the company installed its toll-free service number, nearly half of all customer inquiries to Clairol were in the form of letters. Responding to all of them, needless to say, was expensive. The letters often contained only sketchy information and required additional correspondence between the company and customers to clarify and resolve the problems. Obviously, the telephone allows far more effective communications: all details are obtained at once, which usually results in prompt and satisfactory responses to customers' complaints.

DIGITAL EQUIPMENT CORPORATION

DEC decided its direct sales force could be more efficient if it concentrated on making new sales rather than on taking orders from existing customers. DEC installed a toll-free inbound number for customers, whose phone orders are shipped within 24 hours. The field sales force is now free for new business.

ECKLERS CORVETTE PARTS

Ecklers has a biannual direct-mail catalog. Recipients of the catalog were notified that a toll-free inbound number had been installed to take service calls and orders of Corvette parts, which are hard to find for older models. As a result, calls to the company increased from 1,700 to 7,000 per month, with two key benefits: a significant amount of cross-selling took place, which created new business, and customer service improved significantly.

KELLY SPRINGFIELD

Kelly, a tire manufacturer, serves tire dealers. It talks with 400 Kelly dealers each day on incoming lines. The company also makes 3,000 outgoing calls each week. Kelly uses telemarketing to speed order processing and educate dealers and customers on Kelly products. Kelly maintains regular contact with customers through systematic telemarketing, thereby developing personal relationships with each of its dealers. This personal attention, in turn, fosters brand loyalty in this very competitive field.

DELAWARE VALLEY WHOLESALE FLORIST

Delaware Valley calls on 600 florists each day across the nation. The company's flowers, which may be cut in Holland on a Tuesday, are shipped to florists in the United States by Wednesday morning and delivered to customers by that evening. This market requires a swift and reliable sales medium. Only telemarketing is fast enough to keep pace.

Starting Small

Although these examples are from large, relatively well-known companies, telemarketing works just as well for small companies. One creative example that comes to mind involves a single-plant manufacturer of furnaces for mobile homes. The company ships them to mobile-home plants around the country. Each truckload of furnaces originally consisted of a single type (gas, oil, or electric) and usually a single model or size.

The chronic problem the company faced was sending out semitrailers that were only partially loaded. The solution was to train the warehouse counter clerks to do basic telemarketing. When a partial load was scheduled, the clerks called all the mobile home manufacturers on the planned route and attempted to make enough additional sales to fill it. This effort substantially increased the efficiency of the company's trucking operation and its market share.

In another example, a small discount investment-advisory firm set up a marketing program to acquire new accounts through telemarketing. Over $10 million was brought under management in the first year alone. The firm started with two telemarketers and ended the year with five.

As these examples indicate, it does not take a lot of telemarketing sales representatives (TSRs) to make an impact. Here's what five TSRs can do:

6 hours per day × 5 TSRs = 30 hours per day
30 hours per day × 5 days a week = 150 hours a week
150 hours/week × 20 dialings/hour = 3,000 dialings/week
3,000 dialings/week × 50 weeks = 150,000 dialings/year

Even after taking into account that as many as four or five dialings are often required to reach one decision maker, the fact remains that five TSRs alone can make sales presentations to 30,000 to 40,000 prospects a year. The point is that relatively small telemarketing centers, with one to five TSRs, can have a substantial impact on your sales.

What Telemarketing Cannot Do

Telemarketing is not a cure-all for every marketing problem. If a product or service fails because it does not satisfy customer needs, telemarketing will be as futile as any other marketing medium. Let me give you an actual example.

I was once approached to develop and test a telemarketing program for a company that sold impulse items to convenience stores. These were little things like jewelry, key chains, disposable lighters, car fresheners, etc. In the industry, they are affectionately referred to as "trinkets 'n' trash."

Once we attacked the market, we quickly learned why telemarketing could not deliver:

- At one time, convenience stores were "mom and pop" operations. Now they are primarily chains. This means there are few buying decision makers in the stores anymore. Sales are made at the headquarters by annual bids requested by professional purchasing agents who are not accessible to telemarketers.

- If store displays sell out, clerks are instructed to remove them from view or pitch them. They had no authority to reorder, and calling them was futile.

- Route salesmen, in most cases, set up and refilled displays. They additionally cleaned the shelving space and dusted the merchandise. In other words, the stores counted on some maintenance assistance as part of the sale. Unfortunately, a telemarketer cannot help with this function.

Although this telemarket project as a whole was unsuccessful in capturing a market for my client, it did provide enough research to develop a marketing plan that worked.

It also illustrates three other important points about the use of telemarketing. First, it is flexible. We started as telephone sales representatives (TSRs) and ended up as tele-researchers. Tattoo the following on your forehead: "Never waste a call!" If you or one of your TSRs gets someone on the phone willing to talk about business, draw out as much information as possible. This attitude led to a clear understanding of the structure of this particular industry and what my client needed to do to successfully compete.

Second, test before you commit. If this company had invested in an expensive telemarketing center and a large staff before it learned how the industry worked, it would have regretted its decision. Start small; grow as fast as your knowledge and experience permits.

Last—and this is specifically directed to all of you readers who will manage telemarketing centers—stay close to your TSRs when a new project is starting. Monitor as many calls as possible. Be ready to join a conversation if it sounds like it is yielding valuable new information that your TSR may not be prepared to handle. You should have a better overview of the project from talking with the principals and/or planning the project. This can make a real difference in understanding what the subject is trying to tell you. Therefore, be ready to do some talking yourself whenever warranted. Later, we'll discuss silent monitoring equipment and barge-in features of telephone systems.

Telemarketing cannot function in a vacuum. To be successful, it must be integrated into your firm's total marketing mix. For example, before a newly developed product can be sold successfully via telemarketing, it inevitably requires a broad base of customer awareness. Advertisements must be run, brochures mailed, press releases distributed, and so on. In short, whatever is normally required to introduce a product must be done before telemarketing efforts can be expected to pay off.

Further, telemarketing is not effective with every prospective customer, any more than direct mail, conventional selling, or any other type of merchandising. Consumers, for example, frequently consider a call at home in the evening as an invasion of privacy and become annoyed. This is one reason telemarketing to individual consumers is always far more difficult than to businesses. Finally, telemarketing is a sales and marketing medium, like any other business effort, and is affected by the quality of management. Over the years, I've developed what I call the "Deadly Management Sins of Telemarketing," which may help you avoid a few pitfalls.

THIRTEEN DEADLY SINS

1. Lack of Top Management's Commitment

If the head honcho isn't in your corner, you're in trouble. This is true of just about every corporate endeavor. Spend as much time as necessary selling your leader on the value—and there is plenty—of telemarketing. Be very specific. Be very prepared. Plan. Set budgets. Goals. Job descriptions. Equipment specifications. Reference guide (Chapter 10). The works—don't hold back. Delay the project if you don't have total commitment; it's that important!

Why all the paranoia? Telemarketing can be so powerful, it often threatens key executives. At the same time, it has its detractors, its malpracticers, and its scandals. A solid, well-thought-out plan can be killed by mudslingers. Prepare for the worst, particularly if you are presenting a new approach in a stiff corporate atmosphere.

2. Foggy Goals and Measurements

Every sales or marketing effort must be effective. It's the nature of professional salespeople to prove their worth; telemarketing is no different. At some point, you'll be called on to detail your achievements. To do this, you need reasonable and achievable goals for all your TSRs and a way to evaluate their performance. Build these into your program from the very beginning. We'll discuss how in later chapters.

3. Underestimating Telemarketing's Capabilities

I used to work with an AT&T rep who asked clients just getting into telemarketing if they could handle a 100 percent increase in sales. I initially thought he was using hyperbole to sell, until I learned how to telemarket.

If telemarketing is right for your product and market (two big ifs), wonderful things happen. But you never want to disappoint customers, so be prepared for the best as well as the worst.

Another area, which I'll detail later, is estimating the number of sales contacts a telemarketer can make in the course of a week or a month. You don't want to get your telemarketing operation up and running, only to run out of people to call!

4. Bucking Industry Procedures

I previously described an actual example of how a telemarketing program failed because it wasn't suited for a specific industry. There is no excuse for a marketer not knowing all the pressure points of his/her industry. Telemarketing is very flexible and can be useful in most instances, but not all. By the time you finish this book, you won't make this mistake, as long as you do your homework.

5. Suspicious, Uninvolved Field Sales Force

Many of the best salespeople I know have one unnerving characteristic: insecurity. The best salespeople feel they must go out each day and prove themselves over and over again. It must be this drive that helps them withstand rejection and gives them the tenacity to overcome all kinds of obstacles.

The negative side is they can turn against your telemarketing effort if they feel threatened. Are they going to be replaced with inexpensive telemarketers? A personal sales call costs approximately $250, while a telemarketing sales call is less than one-tenth as much. Now, I'm not equating the two, but this thought can occur to a sales force or sales manager. Especially when you consider how the cost of travel is going up and the cost of telephoning down.

I once worked with a company that wanted to free up more time for its field sales force to open new accounts. Marketing management decided to create a telemarketing center to service existing accounts. They directed the traveling salespeople to call only on new accounts and leave the old ones to the telemarketers. To enforce and motivate the new approach, the field people were to receive no commissions on reorders but higher ones on new business.

What did the salespeople do? They went to their old customers and accepted reorders, but turned them in with new account numbers. The company computer accepted the bogus accounts and paid commissions. It didn't take long before the whole sales system was in knots.

My point is that you need to anticipate the impact on a field sales force when you do your initial planning. Get them involved early on. Make them part of the plan. Sell them just as hard as you sell top management. There are many, many benefits telemarketing provides to field sales, as we'll discuss later. Determine what they are specifically for your people, and spell it out to them clearly.

6. No Ongoing Supervision

People left without direction or a leader are often like rudderless ships. Here's a good example. I set up a one-person telemarketing center for a manufacturer of livestock equipment. The objective was to contact each of their dealers monthly and take inbound orders.

The TSR was well trained on outbound sales techniques and provided a comprehensive reference guide. When she arrived at the company, she spent a week in manufacturing and another in service—not a bad idea.

Then she was given a desk outside the sales manager's office. He had not been involved in any of the planning or training, nor did he know what she was supposed to do. She was provided a list of dealers and told to start calling. The sales manager never paid any attention.

About six weeks into the program, I got a call from the president (he had set the whole project up). He said the TSR was supporting herself by generating service and replacement parts sales, but was making few new product sales. What went wrong?

It took about 10 minutes of listening to determine the problem. She'd call a dealership, ask for the manager by name and say, "Are you having any problems today?" She had picked this up in the service department and the dealers had responded positively, so she continued to do it. When she first started, she told me she had tried to push a new hog-watering system, but no one was interested. I asked her who she had called. When she told me, I knew she had been calling an area that raises cattle, not hogs. There would never be any interest. The rejection caused her to fall back on problem solving as a safe way to go.

It didn't take much to get this TSR back on the sales track. The point is that telemarketers, for the most part, want and respond well to close supervision, unlike most field salespeople. If you hire a staff and leave them on their own, you're going to regret it. Daily meetings, formal or informal, pay big dividends.

7. Poor Hiring Procedures
We'll discuss this in detail in the chapter on staffing. The key is to know in advance what your telemarketing staff will be up against—cold-calling, sale closing, customer service and sales upgrading, surveying, etc.—before you hire. Also, screen all prospective TSRs by phone first; that's the first impression they'll make on your customers and prospects.

8. Unsuitable Compensation Program
What gets paid for gets done. If you pay based on the number of dialings, you get a lot of them. I don't know about results.

9. Inappropriate Work Area
All too often, the telemarketing center is an afterthought—nobody planned for it when space was allotted. Don't let this happen. Nothing fancy is required, but the work areas must communicate to the TSRs that they are an important part of your marketing and sales effort.

10. Weak Support Staff

Do you want your TSRs on the phone 50 percent, 75 percent, or 100 percent of the time? Any arrangement can work, but planning and forethought is required. TSRs need a lot of clerical and supervisory backup; lists need to be acquired and sorted by time zone, and telephone numbers added; follow-up letters, brochures, etc., have to be written, personalized, generated, and mailed.

11. New Sales Syndrome

Telemarketing managers often get caught up in the search for new customers and forget the old. At an investment firm we've done a lot of work for, we found that calls to closed or dormant accounts are the most productive. It's a whole lot cheaper to keep an old client than to find a new one.

12. Campaigns du Jour

Most TSRs like reasonably structured routines. They want to be comfortable and familiar with the product they are selling. If you constantly introduce one new campaign or offer after another, your TSRs will not get into a sales rhythm.

13. Informational Black Holes

These are areas that TSRs are not trained to handle. They include unexpected, serious questions that severely shake their confidence in their ability or question the company's integrity. Let's say you're a TSR at General Motors, and you start getting calls about the outboard gas tanks on certain pickup truck models. Prepared TSRs can handle this situation by explaining how the trucks passed all safety tests and the incidence of fires is lower than other types of accidents. If you have a problem, bring it out of the closet and show it to your people. Teach them how to deal with it. Otherwise, they'll be caught offguard and their unpreparedness will damage your company's reputation.

Telemarketing in Different Selling Situations

The next examples illustrate the effective use of telemarketing in various selling and business situations. They are intended to provide ideas on how telemarketing can be used in your company.

MANUFACTURERS WHO SELL DIRECTLY TO PRODUCT CONSUMERS OR END-USERS

The term *product* is used broadly to include goods and services. A mine that supplies sulfur to chemical manufacturers, a manufacturer of automobile parts, a subassembler for manufacturers, a nonstore marketer selling clothing via catalog, a newsletter publisher, even a doctor or lawyer—all can use telemarketing effectively.

In these situations, telemarketing provides the communication link between company and customers. The mine operator uses it to check on customer inventory levels, to keep up with what competitors are charging, and to search for new prospects.

The automobile parts manufacturer uses it to expedite customer orders, handle customer problems, ensure that subassemblers have adequate inventories, explore new products or parts for related industries, and conduct market research to determine if it can expand into the replacement market.

The nonstore clothing marketer makes excellent use of inbound toll-free phone service by providing an 800 number in its catalogs. The marketer thus receives immediate feedback on every mailing and has a chance to both upgrade each call-in order and develop greater rapport with its customers. If the marketer chooses, it can make outbound calls to prime customers and offer specials based on previous buying habits.

Publishers who sell directly to readers have traditionally used direct mail. But they are beginning to use telemarketing, especially if their publications are written for busy executives whose secretaries are apt to trash such mail.

Telemarketing also is very useful in obtaining changes of sub-scriber addresses (inbound) or as a follow-up to renewal efforts. For example, when renewal calls are made, the telemarketer often learns that the subscriber has moved to another job. The telemar-keter then can attempt to sell the publication to the person's replacement and learn where the ex-subscriber has gone. This kind of aggressive selling, which converts one kind of call into another, cannot be done as economically any other way.

Publishers of subscription publications also prize the valuable editorial feedback they can obtain from telemarketing. Editorial problems can be discovered quickly and changed before damage results. Was a popular column dropped? Is the new design pleas-ing? Are recent format changes effective? These types of questions can be answered quickly.

Professionals, including lawyers, doctors, accountants, etc., should have at least one staff member trained in telemarketing to handle incoming calls. This person should know what the firm can and cannot do and be able to quickly build the confidence of callers regarding the skills and experience of the professionals. Here are a few examples.

Let's say you are a radiologist who wants to build your mammogram business. All you need do is run an ad offering a free copy of the American Medical Association booklet on mammograms in the women's section of your local newspapers—"Call for a free copy." Your practice does this as a public service, which it is.

When interested parties respond, your receptionist tells them about a mini-seminar you are offering once a month on Tuesday evenings. A staff doctor, preferably female, is available to answer all their questions. A tour of your facilities is included. This low-key "show 'n' tell" sales approach will build business. The key is having someone genuinely interested in helping people answer the phone.

What if you're an accountant? Then consider a booklet on the 10 most overlooked tax deductions for individuals or businesses, depending on your target market. Also, accountants, take note that the U.S. Supreme Court knocked down a Florida law prohibiting accountants from telemarketing. Lawyers can offer booklets on divorce, real estate, or whatever their specialty might be. Engineering or construction firms might offer something like "Everything You Need to Know Before Building."

Personally, I've written many "all you need to know" brochures about commodity trading, options, financing, leasing, etc. They really work. A variation is "what you must do before" you write a will, learn to fly, etc. I'm not sure you'll find an easier way to uncover prospects, and telemarketing qualifies and closes them for you.

MANUFACTURERS WHO SELL TO RETAILERS OR DEALERS

This sales situation has a middleman: the manufacturer sells to someone (a retailer) who resells the product to the ultimate consumer. Some examples are a tire producer specializing in the replacement market, personal computer manufacturers whose systems are sold in retail stores, and producers of perishable foods sold through supermarkets. All can, and do, use telemarketing to enhance the efficiency of their normal channels of distribution.

With the middleman added to the distribution chain, the distance between producer and end-user is substantially greater and the sales effort more complex. The manufacturer in this market situation must compete not only for the retailer's attention but also for the attention of the retailer's customers, the ultimate consumers or users of its products. And if the product requires postsale service, the manufacturer is one significant step removed from what might be an unhappy customer.

In addition, the manufacturer may not always be satisfied with the retailer's marketing efforts. In fact, the objectives of the manufacturer may not be the same as those of its retailers. Retailers are interested in selling as much as they can of whatever brand is "hot" at the time, and, unfortunately, this may not be the manufacturer's brand.

The point is that a gulf exists between the producer of a product and the product's ultimate customer that requires continuous bridging. Telemarketing is an effective and efficient way to ensure that loyal customers are kept that way and that new customers are created, regardless of the divergence between the manufacturer and retailer objectives.

As we consider the following examples of creative telemarketing in this particular real-life sales situation, the versatility and power of this medium become even more apparent.

Example 1

A manufacturer sets up one task force of telemarketers to perform order-taking on regular accounts, thereby freeing the sales force to set up new dealerships. This in itself improves the service regular customers receive. A second group of telemarketers is used to activate dormant accounts and to service marginal accounts. Besides generating additional sales, this effort gives these accounts the feeling that they have a "personal friend" they can turn to at the manufacturer's home office or regional headquarters.

The objective of both telemarketing groups is to build brand loyalty for the manufacturer among all the dealers. Since dealers generally can sell any brand, the manufacturer must give them a special reason to sell its particular brand. Telemarketing provides an important edge in this kind of situation.

The manufacturer in our example can also use a third group of telemarketers to handle end-user customer complaints. The company's retail ads spell out the product's warranty and provides a toll-free number for additional information. The 800 number also is displayed on the company's sales literature and on the warranty cards received by customers at the time of purchase.

The objective of the third group of telemarketers is to defuse negative word-of-mouth comments by dissatisfied customers and to promote positive word-of-mouth advertising. Also, by recording and tracking complaints, the manufacturer is alerted quickly to dealers who are not living up to the company's specified sales and service standards.

Example 2

Computer companies have to deal with the same problem: building brand loyalty among dealers. However, computer manufacturers have an additional problem: their product is very complicated. Retail floor salespeople can master most products they sell. This is not always true, however, when it comes to such complex products as computer hardware and software.

If you were in the market for a personal computer and one manufacturer offered a toll-free phone number for immediate help and the other did not, which would you be more comfortable buying? If you were encouraged to make a call or two before you made your computer purchase, and you found the person on the other end to be friendly, encouraging, courteous, and knowledgeable, how much would this influence your selection? And finally, if the technical assistance provided by phone was free for the first 90 days and available at nominal cost after that, would this make a difference to you?

Example 3

Producers of perishable foods also have unique problems telemarketing can address. Consider, for example, the actual case of a small producer of high-quality sausages and cold cuts sold in a very localized market area. The company wished to become a regional supplier. The only way for the company to obtain access to the broader regional market was to have its products accepted by a regional food store chain. Since its products sold at a premium price, discount chains were immediately eliminated as prospects. The top-of-the-line food store chain in the area was the best prospect.

New equipment doubled its sausage-making capacity, but the company could not afford to hire a field salesperson or invest in any large-scale promotional or advertising effort. Furthermore, the targeted food store chain gave only marginal discretionary buying to its individual store managers.

The sausage company's first step was to send a representative to the food chain's headquarters. A polite meeting resulted in general approval of the company's sample products, but the representative was told that demand from the marketplace dictated the brands the stores stocked. If some of the chain's individual store managers wanted to test-market the product, it was entirely up to them; however, headquarters would not provide a list of the managers' names.

The sausage company decided to initiate a telemarketing effort. The owner's secretary, who has a good voice and telephone personality, became the entire telemarketing center. The first objective was to develop the prospect list. Thus the secretary-turned-telemarketer called every one of the chain's stores in the targeted area and obtained the managers' names.

She then called each one to offer samples, which were sent to their homes, because some of the products required cooking before eating. A second round of calls was made a week after the samples were delivered to obtain their reaction and to offer a special 50 percent discount on the first order, some point-of-purchase material, and an in-store demonstration. The promotions would be staggered over the introductory period, depending on how many stores were involved and the size of each.

The final phase of the telemarketing campaign was the most critical, since, to get repeat sales, the company had to create demand for its products at the consumer level. To accomplish this, the sausage maker included a coupon for a free sausage cookbook that customers could order via a toll-free number. This gave the company a chance to reach the ultimate customers directly and to stimulate demand by stressing quality and purity. Once demand was established and rapport built with the store managers, the company was able to sell other products to the stores.

MANUFACTURERS WHO SELL TO WHOLESALERS

This channel of distribution places two or more intermediaries between the producer and the ultimate consumer or user. These middlemen might be agents, distributors, jobbers, or service companies in addition to the retailers. As a rule, the more steps between a company and the end users of its products, the more helpful telemarketing becomes. The reason is simple: telemarketing provides companies with fast and accurate feedback, thereby eliminating the need to wait for problems to percolate through three or four distribution levels.

Telemarketing can be used to learn what is happening currently in the distribution chain. Many of the strategies and tactics described in the manufacturer-to-retailer situation apply here as well. One common approach that is both relatively inexpensive and simple to implement is including a warranty card with products, which encourages customers to register or report problems to the manufacturer by calling a toll-free service number.

Here is a typical case. A manufacturer of tool chests for mechanics sold them through independent sales representatives to jobbers who, in turn, distributed them to retailers, who sold them to automobile mechanics. The jobbers resisted revealing the names of their retailers for fear that the manufacturer would preempt their sales efforts and sell directly to their retail accounts. Because of such tight-lipped jobbers, the manufacturer could not tell callers (prospective customers) the location of the nearest retail outlet. The manufacturer had a toll-free service phone line but could not fully utilize it. It also included a warranty card with each tool chest, but the returned warranties were never processed.

How did telemarketing help this situation? First, the manufacturer had to gain the trust of the jobbers. The jobbers perform the functions of warehousing the product in the territory, making sales calls on the retailers, delivering the products to the retailers (and sometimes the end user), and performing some low-level service/warranty work. By executing a written agreement with the jobbers promising not to sell at retail, the manufacturer convinced the jobbers to release their lists of retailers.

Once this was done, the manufacturer included an inbound toll-free number in display ads that offered to provide customers with the names and addresses of the nearest retailers. Also, upon the return of the completed warranty cards, a small gift was sent to customers; this provided the company with an opportunity to capture demographic information about purchasers as well as their phone numbers for future use. A representative sampling of these respondents was called to obtain feedback on everything from product quality to pricing. And, since the leads from the display ads were passed on to the jobbers for follow-up, representative samples of the inquiries were periodically surveyed to determine if the jobbers were contacting the respondents.

The manufacturer also anonymously called the jobbers' salespeople to learn firsthand how they responded to inquiries about the product. Were they knowledgeable? Were they representing the manufacturer in a professional manner?

As the examples indicate, the more complicated a company's sales system, the more integral and necessary its telemarketing program, and the more pressing the need to stay abreast of activity on all levels of the marketing channel. This is especially true for products requiring after-sales service or support.

Product Life Cycle and Telemarketing

The stage a particular product has reached in its life cycle often can determine the nature and extent of the telemarketing tactics and strategies to be explored. Mature, well-established products, for example, require less extensive telephone sales presentations. In fact, very often they may require only an inbound toll-free number to facilitate easy reordering. For these products, the sole marketing objective may to be maintain current market share. Telemarketing, of course, can help achieve this.

Newly introduced products, on the other hand, require an entirely different set of telephone tactics. The TSRs must spend the time to describe the product to prospective customers, to enumerate its benefits, and to create interest in it. The telemarketer must convince customers that the new product is worth the investment. Before a sale is finalized, three or more calls are often required, and product specifications, photographs, samples, and background material may have to be sent.

Can Your Product Be Sold Through Telemarketing?

Stocks, bonds, computers, life insurance, jewelry, and cement are among the products sold today via telemarketing. But there is only one sure way to answer this question, and that is to test it, either on your own or through a professional telemarketing service agency. Probably the easiest, most accurate, and least disruptive approach is to use an outside telemarketing firm that employs professional TSRs. If the test produces promising results, a telemarketing program on a small scale can be set up in-house.

To use telemarketing is a simple economic decision. All too often, managers are distracted from effective telemarketing by the ever-present side issues: What are my customers going to think? Will they be irritated by a call? Can my product be fairly represented? My advice to you is to try it. Find out for yourself. Many of these same arguments were raised about direct mail 20 years ago, and today just about everybody uses it. The same will soon be true of telemarketing.

Time and again, I hear the complaint that "my product is too complicated" (or too expensive or too specialized) to be sold by telemarketing! I generally ask in response: "Do your salespeople have phones in their offices?" Invariably, the answer is yes. My rejoinder is, "Then you are already using telemarketing. All you need to do at this point is organize the process."

The Unique Characteristics of Telemarketing

2

Although telemarketing shares several characteristics similar to those of direct-mail marketing and person-to-person sales, it is, nevertheless, a unique marketing resource. Understanding its features further clarifies its potential uses within a marketing/sales program and, at the same time, sheds light on its particular economic structure.

Telemarketing is similar to direct-mail marketing in that it is a high-volume, promotional sales tool, and, as such, works best when applied to a somewhat large and accessible market—one with plentiful customer and prospect lists. As with direct mail, telemarketing results can be measured exactly. Telemarketing, however, differs markedly from direct mail in at least three important areas: (1) in the amount of detail the sales message can deliver; (2) in its ability to provide personal, after-sales support;

(3) and in its capacity to cope effectively with reactions to sales messages.

Limits of the Telemarketing Sales Message

A typical direct-mail package can include numerous promotional pieces. Multiple-page sales letters, descriptive brochures, samples, order forms, lift letters, and endorsements are typical components of direct-mail packages. When properly executed, the direct-mail sales message is comprehensive. The package provides all of the information anyone would need in order to make an informed buying decision.

Telemarketing, by contrast, is usually restricted to a brief sales message. There is not enough time during a typical call to present the complete case for a product or service, nor is the medium right for extensive sales presentations; people are just not that patient.

The point is clear: telemarketing, when used for direct solicitation, works best for products or services that can be described simply and succinctly. This statement, however, should not be interpreted to mean that the product or service being telemarketed must be simplistic. That is not the case at all. When a complex engineering device is sold to engineers, there is no need for elaborate presentation. Similarly, there is no need for comprehensive presentations of case books to law firms, complex subassembly work to manufacturers, chemical compounds to industrial chemists, and so forth.

The telemarketing sales message, therefore, is not limited so much by the characteristics of the product or service as by the degree to which that product or service is known and understood by prospective customers. This fact leads to two important concepts in telemarketing: the supremacy of the prospect list and the fact that telemarketing is just one part of the entire marketing mix. As such, it must be coordinated with your company's other promotional, advertising, and sales efforts.

Telemarketing's Biggest Advantage

Despite the relative comprehensiveness and sleek packaging of direct mail, as an advertising medium it is fundamentally passive. The prospect can easily decide not to open a direct-mail package. Even if he or she does decide to open it, there is no guarantee it will be read.

Telemarketing, on the other hand, is far more demanding. It presses for a hearing and cannot be discarded without being opened. Furthermore, if a name on the prospect list is incorrect, the telemarketer can inquire as to the name of the person he/she should be talking with. Direct mail addressed to the wrong person seldom reaches its destination.

Telemarketing is extremely flexible, and its ability to cope with a broad range of individuals is unmatched. Well-trained TSRs can immediately counter specific objections that a customer or prospect may pose during the course of a sales presentation. Or, your TSR can take an order on the spot. Moreover, telemarketing allows a quick adjustment to the circumstances at hand. If the sales presentation in a telephone campaign is not working, telemarketing activity can be halted instantly and a new script devised and tested. Once a direct-mail piece has been dropped in the mail, misconceptions, miscalculations, and errors cannot be rectified.

Telemarketing and Conventional Person-to-Person Selling

Many of the selling skills a professional field sales representative develops are also used by telemarketers. Their respective jobs are, in large part, the same—i.e., to sell. The circumstances in which they interact with customers are different, however, and require different strategies.

Field sales representatives make face-to-face sales calls, while TSRs are restricted to telephone communications. One big advantage of face-to-face selling is the ability to interpret and respond to nonverbal signals—e.g., body language. There is also the importance of the presence of the sales representative. Additionally, a personal sales call can go on for an hour or more.

However, what the field sales representatives achieve with their presence, TSRs can make up for in the number of customers or prospects they can contact in the same amount of time. Since the average telemarketing call lasts only 2½ to 5 minutes and no travel is required, the TSR can "visit" 30 to 50 prospects in a single day. Field representatives, on the other hand, may only be able to make four or five appointments. TSRs can also make up for their "lack of physical presence" by skilled questioning and enthusiasm. It is much easier for TSRs to get back to visit customers, so they do it more frequently.

Within the marketing mix are clear and distinct uses for direct mail, conventional selling, and telemarketing. They are complementary, not mutually exclusive, sales approaches. Understanding the advantages, disadvantages, strengths, and weaknesses of each allows you to develop highly effective marketing programs. We will discuss this issue in more detail in Chapter 8, "Integrating Telemarketing into the Marketing Mix."

Comparative Analysis of the Economics of Telemarketing

Telemarketing can cost four to six times as much as direct-mail marketing, yet it can produce response rates five or even ten times greater. Compared to personal selling on a completed-call basis, telemarketing costs generally average about one-tenth as much.

The analysis below compares the economics of telemarketing to direct mail.

Direct-Mail Costs to Reach a Sales Goal of $65,000

Assumptions:

- The product being offered has a selling price of $65.

- Bad debt is estimated at 2 percent of gross sales and returned merchandise at 1.5 percent.

- List rental costs are assumed to be $70 per thousand names mailed and a list of 66,667 names will be used.

- Design, printing, and typesetting costs of the package are $300 per thousand names mailed.

- A 1.5 percent response rate (the percent of contacted prospects who buy) would result in the sale of 1,000 units (66,667 names × 1.5%).

- Mailing house costs are $25 per thousand.

- Postage is $167 per thousand.

- Cost of goods sold is 15 percent of gross sales.

- Fulfillment and order processing are $1.25 per unit sold.

	Direct-Mail Profit/(Loss)
Sales	$65,000
Bad debt	($1,300)
Returned merchandise	($975)
Net sales	$62,745
List rental	($4,667)
Design, typesetting, and printing	($20,000)

Mailing house	($1,667)
Postage	($11,138)
Costs of goods	($9,750)
Fulfillment/order processing	($1,250)
Total costs	($48,472)
Profit before overhead and taxes	$14,273
Profit margin	22%

Telemarketing Costs to Reach a Sales Goal of $65,000

Assumptions:

- The product has a selling price of $65.

- A prospect list consisting of 6,250 names is used, and each number is attempted three times, for a total of 18,750 dialings (3 calls × 6,250 prospects = 18,750 dialings).

- Four TSRs are used; each averages 15 dialings per hour for total hours of 1,250 (18,750 dialings ÷ 15 dialings per hour = 1,250 hours).

- Long-distance billing charges are no more than 50 percent of total TSR labor hours:

  Actual billable hours: 625 (1,250 total labor hours × 50%)

  Long-distance rate of $0.20 per minute: $7,500 (625 × 60 ÷ $0.20)

- TSR salary, incentives, and benefits are $9.60 per hour for total TSR costs of $12,000 ($9.60 × 1,250 hours = $12,000).

- Of the prospect list of 6,250 names, 5,000 (or 80 percent) are reachable and 20 percent respond by purchasing the product. Unit sales are 1,000 (5,000 × 20%).

- Bad debt is 2 percent of gross sales, while returned merchandise is 15 percent.

- Cost of goods is 15 percent of the selling price.

- List rental, including phone numbers, is $120 per thousand names.

- Fulfillment is $1.25 per shipped item.

	Telemarketing Profit/(Loss)
Sales	$65,000
Bad debt	($1,300)
Returned merchandise	($9,750)
Net sales	$53,950
List rental	($750)
Cost of goods	($9,750)
Fulfillment	($1,250)
Salary and incentives	($12,000)
Phone charges	($7,500)
Total costs	($31,250)
Profit before overhead and taxes	$22,700
Profit margin	34.9%

The results of this analysis points to three intriguing economic aspects of telemarketing:

1. To attain identical sales goals, based on our likely response assumptions, telemarketing required less than one-tenth of the prospect universe required by direct mail (a customer list of 6,250 names for telemarketing versus 66,667 for direct mail).

2. Returned merchandise in the telemarketing model was assumed at 15 percent compared to 1.5 percent for direct mail. In some telemarketing situations, however, even a 15 percent returned merchandise rate might be considered low. Returned merchandise in consumer telemarketing can reach as high as 25 percent. This is because a decision on the part of the prospect to accept a telemarketing offer is often made quickly, without any examination of the product. There is no brochure to peruse, no samples, and so on. Another reason is the pressure on prospects to accept a person-to-person appeal, which comes simply from the personal nature of phone calls.

3. By far the most intriguing insight to be drawn from our analyses is the high level of operating leverage available from telemarketing, which often can lead to gross margins or incremental sales of 50 percent or better.

For instance, if TSRs in this example (collectively) could make three additional calls per hour, they would accomplish an additional 3,750 dialings during the 1,250 labor hours devoted to this campaign. Assuming it takes three attempts to reach a prospect and that of the 80 percent eventually reached, 20 percent will buy the product, the additional calls result in 200 incremental sales. Since these sales would be made without incurring additional costs, the additional profit calculates as follows:

	Telemarketing Incremental Profit/(Loss)
Sales	$13,000
Bad debt	($260)
Returned merchandise	($1,950)

Net sales	$10,790
List rental	($120)
Cost of goods	($1,950)
Incentives	($100)
Fulfillment	($250)
Total costs	($2,420)
Profit before overhead and taxes	$8,370
Incremental profit margin	64.4%

The incremental profit per sale would be $43.31 per unit sold ($8,662 divided by 200 units) as opposed to $24.16 per unit sold ($24,162 divided by 1,000 units) achieved in the initial campaign. Overall, this would drive down the cost of sales considerably for the total effort and improve the gross margin handily. It is this argument that justifies the automation or computerization of telemarketing, because it can double the effectiveness of your TSRs. We'll talk more about this later.

The limits, efficiencies, and economics of telemarketing have been the subject of this brief but extremely important chapter. The insights achieved by examining the unique characteristics of telemarketing should be kept in mind, since these ideas inevitably form the basis of all carefully considered applications of telemarketing. Additional discussions of telemarketing economics can be found in chapters 5 and 7.

3

Selecting and Preparing the Customer Prospect List for Telemarketing

Without question, the customer prospect list is the single most important element in any telemarketing effort. List selection for telemarketing—and *any* form of direct marketing, for that matter—has more to do with its success or failure than any other single factor. Telemarketing professionals attribute 70 percent of the success of every telemarketing campaign to the quality of the list. The remaining 30 percent is usually attributed to both the effectiveness of the TSRs (20 percent) and the efficiency of the telecommunications/automation equipment (10 percent).

Types of Prospect Lists

There are two basic types of lists: compiled and responsive (the latter is sometimes referred to as behavioral). Compiled lists are names taken from sources of some sort—a phone book or membership directory, for example. Responsive/behavioral lists, on the other hand, are composed of names of people who have previously responded to a type of promotion similar to the one planned or who bought a product/service that is similar to the one being offered. These lists normally produce more responses than compiled lists. Keep in mind, though, that using lists compiled for business-to-business campaigns work fine, as long as the proper SIC (Standard Industrial Classification) selection is made. Business-to-business lists can be chosen much more accurately, as we'll see.

Renting Lists and Capturing Names

Lists for use in direct mail usually are rented on a single-use basis, and often are seeded with dummy names to ensure that they are not copied or input into a computer and used for unauthorized additional mailings. Names are captured from rented lists by getting the people on the lists to respond to your offer. Those who respond belong to you, and you can mail to them as often as you like in the future without having to pay additional rental fees.

Generally, in direct mail, a new customer list is tested before substantial parts of the budget are committed to its use. If the test is successful, the list may be rented over and over again for as long as it remains productive.

In telemarketing, a prospect list usually is rented only once, since every name on the list is contacted, or at least several attempts are made. Business lists are a little more complicated. Here the TSRs are attempting to qualify prospective buyers to find out whether the person named on the list is in a position to make the buying decision. Often there is no name on the lists, and your TSRs must locate the decision maker. Because this is an "exploratory" approach, TSRs often are referred to someone else within the company. However, once the appropriate name is uncovered, it is yours to keep and use as often as you wish in the future. Again, the original owner of the list is paid only once.

For these reasons, lists sold for telemarketing purposes usually cost two to three times more than the same lists rented for direct mail. If the going rate for a list is $65 per thousand for direct mail, the charge will be $100 to $150 for telemarketing. List owners also want to recover the cost of adding the telephone numbers to their list(s).

The business of creating, managing, and renting lists is an outgrowth of the magazine and direct-mail marketing industries; therefore, many lists do not include telephone numbers. However, this situation has improved dramatically in the last few years. If you plan on using a direct-mail or subscriber list for telemarketing, be sure to check beforehand to make sure it includes telephone numbers. There are economical ways of adding phone numbers, which we'll get to shortly.

Common Sources of Customer Lists

IN-HOUSE SOURCES

Every organization has in-house lists. Some of the common categories of these proprietary lists include active customers, inactive customers, prospects who inquired about a product or service, and referrals from customers or third parties. For example, it is not uncommon for companies to have unprocessed warranty cards on hand. The names on these cards can very easily be converted into telemarketing lists and prospected for additional products or services.

TELEPHONE BOOKS

If you sell to businesses, the *Yellow Pages* can be a rich source of names. List brokers who deal in compiled lists have computerized versions of the *Yellow Pages* from virtually every city in the country. You can even select by size of ad in the *Yellow Pages*, so you choose only the larger, more aggressive retailers. Segments of these lists can be selected according to the product classifications that appear in the front of the telephone directory. Brokers can provide such lists on 3" by 5" cards that include customer phone numbers, or on computer tapes, floppy disks, or CD ROM.

Printed directories of all *Yellow Page* listings by state also are available, as are directories of manufacturers by state. Additionally, telemarketers can sign up for list services that allow direct computer access to various databases. Such services provide free catalogs of the lists they offer, including a count of the names in each product category by state. Addresses for some of these services are in Appendix 1. Also check with local printers. Many have input names from the *Yellow Pages* and other local directories into their computers as a way of stimulating printing sales and are willing to rent or otherwise share them.

Of course, if you sell to retail consumers, the white pages of the telephone directory are a source of names. Copies of directories in cities other than your own often can be obtained from the local telephone company. If not, they can be ordered from the telephone company servicing the geographic area targeted. Cross-directories of cities allow you to select prospects by neighborhood. I always obtain phone books from cities in which I do any volume of business. There are just too many free leads to pass up.

LIST BROKERS

Another important and common source for lists is list brokers. These are professionals who act as intermediaries between companies providing mailing lists and those seeking them. All the major list brokers provide free catalogs of the lists they offer (see Appendix 1 for addresses and phone numbers). Many now specialize in lists for telemarketers.

Also, if your firm does not have the computer capacity or expertise, many list brokerage firms, as well as various computer service agencies, will computerize and maintain your lists for a fee or the rights to market (rent) the list for you. Because the list you use is so critical to the success of any telemarketing effort, this approach warrants serious attention.

ASSOCIATIONS

Directories of professional associations, societies, or clubs are prime sources for prequalified, highly targeted prospect lists. Most local libraries have a copy of the *Encyclopedia of Associations.* Use it to locate organizations to which your current customers belong, since prospective customers also may belong. The *Encyclopedia* provides the names, addresses and telephone numbers of the groups' headquarters, which can be contacted for copies of their lists or directories. For example, the list of doctors is available by the year they graduated and their specialty.

GOVERNMENT

The federal government is another valuable source of prospect lists. The regulatory agencies alone can supply enough names for hundreds of telemarketing campaigns. Contact the agency that regulates the field in which you are selling to find out whether its lists are available. Also, the reference desks of most public libraries have directories that indicate the kinds of government lists available.

OTHER SOURCES

There are myriad alternative lists available for local or regional marketing campaigns. Most communities have a branch of the

Daughters of the American Revolution, a library society, marketing clubs, crafts people, trade groups of all sorts, and local chapters of all kinds of commercial organizations. A good place to start is the chamber of commerce. Also, many churches have directories that are composed of people who share common interests, values, lifestyles, etc.

Street-by-street directories are available from several commercial sources, such as R. L. Polk & Co. (see Appendix 1 for the address). These directories are excellent for canvassing towns or cities one neighborhood at a time. They are often used to obtain numerous consecutive appointments by insurance salespeople in the same neighborhood.

Newspapers can be useful sources of facts about marriages, births, job promotions or changes, and so on. Once you know prospects' names, it's easy to locate their phone numbers.

Most industry trade publications have a buyer's guide issue that includes all the companies supplying goods and services to a given industry. The ads in these magazines also are good sources of prospects if you sell to certain types of vendors, and they always include phone numbers.

Selecting the Right List

Once you have located a variety of sources for lists, how do you decide which ones to use?

First and foremost, study your current customers. List everything you know about them and their behavior on a piece of paper. Here are some of the more common items:

If You Sell Business-to-Business:

1. Company name, account number, and Standard Industrial Classification code

2. Mailing address

3. Shipping address, if different

4. Number of locations

5. Complete phone number

6. Names of buyers by product line

7. Names of assistant buyers or secretaries by product line

8. Names of product specifiers in the case of engineered products

9. Third-party influencers, if applicable

10. Annual volume of purchases of your products

11. Maximum potential annual volume of purchases

12. Credit rating and history

13. Other suppliers used by the company

14. Primary competitor for this account

15. Terms and conditions of sale

16. Pricing schedule or discounts

17. Primary contact at your company

18. Client's normal order/reorder cycle

19. Reason account sold initially

20. Date of last sale

21. Size of last sale and average sale size

22. Customer's gross sales or other measure of size

23. Number of employees

24. Gross income

If You Sell to Consumers:

1. Name/occupation

2. Spouse's name/occupation

3. Address

4. Home and work phone numbers

5. Demographics (available from census tract computer tapes) —

   a. Gender

   b. National origin (computer programs that can classify individuals based on the national origin of their last names)

   c. Age

   d. Marital status

   e. Income or net worth bracket

   f. Number and type of cars

   g. Neighborhood classification

   h. Affiliations

   i. Dependents

   j. Homeowner/renter

6. Psychographics —

   a. Hobbies

   b. Likes and dislikes

   c. Politics

   d. Clubs and other memberships

7. Creditworthiness

8. Buying habits (credit vs. cash)

9. Sales potential for your products/services

The more you know about your customers, the easier it is to find prospects who are similar to them and who are therefore potential customers. This information is useful in describing to list brokers the kind of prospects you seek.

The very first characteristic listed for business telemarketing is the Standard Industrial Classification (SIC) number. All companies in the United States and most foreign countries are assigned a SIC number. Prospect lists using this number can be rented and matched against lists that contain other company characteristics, such as gross sales or number of employees, to further screen the prospect list. You can even screen by credit ratings using data available from Standard & Poor's Register or Dun & Bradstreet. Table 3–1 lists some representative SIC codes and counts (numbers of companies in each classification).

TABLE 3–1

SIC Code	Description	Count
8931A	Accounting services	53,248
6311	Advertising agencies	21,981
1711C	Air-conditioning contractors	39,093
5531	Auto parts & home supply stores	110,431
5463	Bakeries	28,982
8664A	Buddhist temples	290
7399	Business services	104,091
6221A	Commodity brokers	3,187
6141	Credit unions	22,767
8021	Dentists	115,187
5063	Electrical equipment wholesalers	50,156

TABLE 3–1 (continued)

SIC Code	Description	Count
5992	Florists	43,460
5947A	Gift shops	59,973
6512C	Halls & auditoriums	4,697
7349A	Janitorial services	22,633
6699G	Locksmiths	10,918
1389	Oil & gas field services	20,313
5086	Professional equipment wholesalers	36,417
2075	Soybean oil mills	60
7299A	Tax return preparation services	22,276
5921A	Wine retailers	9,252

Source: *The National Business List Catalog,* Market Data Retrieval, 1-800-Mail-Now.

Testing the List

Regardless of how close a fit a list may seem to be for a particular product, it is not wise to rent or buy the list in its entirety before testing at least some portion of it. The exceptions to this rule are, naturally, very small lists and directories.

Testing a list simply involves telemarketing to a segment of test names selected randomly and evaluating the results. The sample should be as fairly representative of the list as possible. In direct-marketing parlance, we are testing for statistical validity; i.e., how much of any list must be tested in order to perform a valid statistical evaluation.

For example, in direct mail, list testing usually begins with a mailing to a representative sample of 5,000 names. If an acceptable level of response is achieved, the list is further tested with a roll-out mailing to no more than 10 times the number of the test (50,000). If those results are favorable, additional roll-outs up to 5 million are justified.

You may be asking how one determines what level of response is needed to justified roll-out mailings. One cannot really know for sure, but a degree of probability can be assigned to the results by using statistical methods (for the mathematically inclined) or by referring to statistical tables known commonly as confidence tables, which can be found in just about any direct-marketing text. Confidence tables assign relative probabilities to different testing levels, usually beginning with a universe of 5,000 names.Fundamentally, the same list-testing principles that apply to direct mail hold true for telemarketing as well. Because telemarketing depends on a series of human interactions that vary from call to call, as opposed to a uniform direct-mail package, test evaluation also must take into account such factors as the hours called, calls completed, number of sales made, and the skill of the TSRs, which vary widely.

Although the probability of roll-out response rates cannot be as neatly determined in telemarketing as in direct mail, the relative value of a list still can be ascertained by testing smaller segments of it. The best test, of course, is whether the promotion makes money or not. The real beauty of telemarketing is that it can be stopped on a dime. Direct mail, once dropped, cannot be halted.

The test should begin with a 50- to 100-hour effort, which, if favorable, would be rolled out to a 200- to 500-hour test, and so on. Assuming a TSR can make 20 dialings an hour, a 100-hour test using a single TSR would require 2,000 names, assuming each name is attempted only once. This, of course, will vary depending on the type of call, the quality of the list, and other variables.

After 50 to 60 hours—two weeks of calling for one TSR—you should begin to develop a feel for the quality of the list, having determined by then the accuracy of phone numbers, the interest level of the prospects, the availability of decision makers, the rate at which they are placing orders, and, finally, whether the list is cost effective.

When considering a new list, it often is worthwhile to test it first with a direct mailing, if this is possible, before committing to use the list for telemarketing purposes. A small segment of prospects, for example, can be tested less expensively using direct mail than telemarketing. If the list works for direct mail, the odds are very much in favor of it also working for telemarketing. Furthermore, a successful direct mailing to the test segment of a list may encourage you to search for other sources of similar names to test that do not include telephone numbers. It may be worth the expense to add phone numbers to a sufficient number of the names on a mail list to allow for an economical telemarketing test. This would especially make sense if only a limited supply of telemarketing lists were available for the product or service you're marketing.

Two words of warning: First, move slowly with new lists, because some unethical list sellers will give you their best names first. These are "hot responders," or names of people who recently responded. As you commit for larger quantities, you get older names, and the connect rate drops sharply. Second, during the test process you'll be tempted to use only your best TSRs, because they are fast learners. Later, when you roll out, you use your whole staff, and the results drop off. Use a fair mix of your TSRs so you can rely on the test results.

Adding Phone Numbers to a List

The least expensive way to add phone numbers to large lists of names is to use a computerized matching service. To do this, however, the list must be on magnetic tape. The cost of the service is about 10 cents for every number added. Most services average a 50 percent success rate.

Other "look-up" services manually use phone directories or directories on microfiche. These companies charge approximately 25 cents for each name searched. To put these charges in perspective, keep in mind that the telephone company's Directory Assistance service charges as much as $1 for each inquiry, and this does not include the costs associated with the telemarketer's staff time in making the calls. Another option, of course, is to obtain directories yourself and have your staff look up the numbers.

Also, many local phone companies now offer direct computer-to-computer access to their phone number databases for an hourly rate. This, of course, would require a computer with communications capabilities. But it's fast, accurate, and up-to-date.

List Enhancement

Besides adding the telephone number, you can enhance your list by matching it with census data. There are companies that specialize in this service. Your names are matched with the data on the tapes to add all kinds of information (age, household income, number/type of car(s), home ownership/rental, ethnic origin of name, number of people in household, value of average home in neighborhood, etc.). If you have a large list, this is an accurate methodology for pinpointing geographic areas or clusters of prospects with characteristics or demographics similar to your best customers.

Database Marketing

As you enhance and test lists, you're building a database of valuable information. The more you know about your customers and how they make buying decisions, the more successful you'll be. That is what database marketing is all about. Telemarketing is extremely valuable in this process, because it can fill in informational gaps and test hypotheses.

I've often used telemarketing as my "reconnaissance platoon" by sending my TSRs out into new sales territories to find out how much potential there is, who the buyers are, and the size and strength of competition. These results are often more reliable than more conventional market research, because my people are asking for orders.

Gathering marketing intelligence, integrating it into your marketing plan, acting on it, constantly updating and enhancing your understanding of your marketplace, then using all this information to treat each customer as a special individual is the essence of database marketing. And no one can do a better job of it than someone who's talking regularly to your customers.

4

Key Issues on Staffing the Telemarketing Center

Staffing a telemarketing center must be approached from both qualitative and quantitative points of view. The former addresses the *kinds* of people that are needed in a telemarketing center; the latter determines the *number* of people needed to meet the center's particular objectives. Both the qualitative and quantitative aspects of telemarketing staffing considerations are covered in this chapter. Chapter 5, "Planning for Higher Telemarketing Productivity," and Chapter 7, "Budgeting the Telemarketing Center," address the quantitative issues, but from different perspectives. Additionaly, inbound centers have some special staffing considerations, which are discussed in Chapter 12.

The Telemarketing Manager

The telemarketing manager holds the crucial and pivotal position in the telemarketing center. This is the person whose commitment and intelligence must be relied upon to manage the program and produce the desired results. What kind of person should the telemarketing manager be? Here are some attributes to consider in the selection process.

- *Sales Training Experience:* Since the telemarketing manager needs to be able to teach the TSRs how to sell, he or she should have selling and training experience.

- *Supervisory Skills:* Prior successful experience in supervising and motivating salespeople is a key prerequisite.

- *Telemarketing Savvy:* Since the telemarketing manager will be responsible for training, coaching, and motivating the TSRs, he or she must have a sound understanding of and experience in all aspects of telemarketing. This includes hardware (headsets, chairs, computers, etc.) and systems (software, phone, etc.).

- *Product/Company Knowledge:* Again, since the manager is the trainer, his or her complete familiarity with the company's products and internal systems is a necessity.

- *Writing Skills:* The manager will occasionally be required to prepare scripts or follow-up letters, or maybe even the reference guide. Additionally, reports will be needed to gain the support of top management.

The obvious choices for promotion within the organization would be the person in charge of the in-house sales or service department, or an assistant in the sales or marketing department who is ready for a new challenge.

Of course, if the center needs only one or two TSRs, a manager is probably not required, since the TSRs can be supervised by someone from the existing management staff.

Deciding How Many TSRs Will Be Adequate

How many TSRs will you need? Here are a couple of rules of thumb for different sales situations.

Full Account Management

If the TSRs are expected to perform full account management, one telephone sales representative would be needed for every 200 to 500 accounts. Full account management means handling all communications with an account, including solving the customer's problems, while continuing to make repeat sales to the account.

An office supply company provides a good example of the full account management approach. A TSR is assigned 200 accounts. She calls each account approximately twice a month to obtain an order. Between these calls, she handles all back orders and invoicing problems and expedites shipments. Additionally, she maintains a complete up-to-date file on each account.

As you might imagine, staffing for full account management requires considering several variables. A lot depends on how much service each account requires, the length of the reorder cycle, the complexity of the product, and the paperwork. If the TSRs use computerized systems, the number of accounts each can handle can be increased by 50-100 percent.

One-Time-Only Sales

If the operation calls for a one-time-only sale to each prospect, one TSR will be needed for every 300 to 1,000 names that are expected to be called per week. Again, keep in mind that this is a ballpark estimate. The actual requirements for a given center would depend on many variables, including how many attempts the TSR is expected to make to reach each person on the list, product seasonality, the quality of the lists, and so forth. One important list-quality consideration is whether names of decision makers are included. If they are not, TSRs must locate the right persons. Naturally, this takes time. The accuracy of phone numbers on the lists also will have an impact on staffing. If every third number on a list is wrong or disconnected, the TSR will work his or her way through the list very quickly—and very unproductively.

In the end, hands-on experience with a specific product in a specific market will be the only true guide for determining staff size. But when starting out, play it safe. Try not to staff the center initially with more than half the total number of TSRs you expect to need when the program is up and running at full speed. Ideally, a start-up center should have at least two TSRs, but no more than five.

Where Are Good TSRs Found?

Are good telemarketers born or made? Telemarketing is a specialized skill. As is true of most jobs, it can be taught to just about anyone of average intelligence who wants to learn. "Naturals" do exist; however, there are many more well-trained journeymen TSRs than there are naturals. The stars or naturals just seem to pop up out of nowhere and outperform everyone else, attracting a lot of attention, but they are the exceptions.

The first place most companies look is the field sales force. Is there an effective and valued field salesperson out there who is burned out on traveling? The good ones are usually excellent on the phone and, therefore, should be considered for telemarketing.

If you are considering converting a field salesperson to a TSR, talk with that person first. Explain the differences between field and phone sales. Try to evaluate the candidate's level of desire.

Determine whether he or she can make a successful transition to telemarketing, because many consider becoming a TSR a demotion. Also, the compensation paid a field salesperson is usually substantially more.

The steps to making a sale in telemarketing are basically the same as for any other kind of sales effort:

1. The needs of the prospect must be uncovered and the product matched to those needs;

2. Enough information about the product must be conveyed to the prospect to make it understood and desired;

3. Objections must be handled; and

4. The order must be closed.

The difference is in how these steps are taken—and some field sales personnel cannot adjust. A good way to test their adaptability is to allow them to try the job for three to six months on a trial basis. The results might justify a permanent transfer.

Other possible candidates are in-house sales and service personnel or a secretary in the sales or marketing department who wants, and can handle, more of a challenge. Often, TSRs can be recruited from the general office pool, where you may find an employee with prior telemarketing background, or simply place an ad similar to the one below on the office bulletin board and/or in the local paper:

Telephone Sales

Need two friendly, persistent people to sell our products over the phone. Requires good communication skills and the ability to maintain records and take orders. Prior experience helpful, but not mandatory. We sell [name of product]. Call Tom McCafferty for an interview. [Company name, company phone number (but no address).]

The Telephone Interview

Always make the first interview a telephone interview even with in-house personnel, if possible. You simply do not want to prejudice yourself with first appearances. Physical appearance is not important in this job. The benefit of the first interview can be enhanced by having a prepared set of questions and a form on which to record your impressions.

The questions generally fall into three categories. The first probes the person's potential for telemarketing. Can he or she talk easily with you, a stranger? Can the candidate paint interesting word pictures? Here are a few questions you may want to ask.

1. Tell me about a recent movie or TV program you've seen and tell me why I would like to have seen it.

2. Describe your car, house, or apartment and tell me why I would like it.

3. Tell me about your last job. What would I have liked or disliked most about it?

4. What's the most interesting experience you've ever had? How would I have benefited from it?

You can use as many questions of this kind as you feel necessary. The point is to get candidates talking, to see how descriptive they are and if they can sell you on whatever they are talking about. Grade them on your understanding and reaction to what they are pitching. Did you visualize the TV program, car, job experience? Were any of the features described converted into benefits? Would you want them to tell you more? Were they enthusiastic?

The second set of questions pertains to the available TSR position and the candidate's past work experience. Here are some sample questions.

1. What telephone selling have you done?

2. What types of jobs have you been most successful at in the past?

3. What made you answer this particular ad?

4. Do you spend much time on the phone at your present job? How about your previous jobs?

Finally, the third category of questions cover basic personnel department information. Here you ask about education, references, and the like.

During the telephone interview, listen carefully to the person's accent. If you sell in only one region of the country, a local, distinctive accent might be a help. But not if it is so strong that it hampers understanding. If you market nationally, try for as neutral an accent as possible. On the back of the interview form, write your first impressions of each telemarketing candidate, using the sample form as a guide. (See Exhibit 4–1.)

After you have completed all the telephone interviews, you should be able to select easily those candidates you want to invite for a personal interview. The personal interview should be conducted just like any other interview for a sales job, except you must keep in mind that appearance is not a factor in determining eligibility.

Take the time during the interview to review a written job description with the candidate. (See Exhibit 4–2.)

Some companies like to conduct psychological tests before or after the personal interview to determine how extroverted or introverted a candidate might be. Good telemarketers are "ambiverts," falling somewhere in the middle—maybe a shade toward the introverted side of the spectrum.

There are some excellent software programs and consulting firms that can help you screen TSR applicants. I've used a pro-

Exhibit 4–1
Telephone Interview Impressions

Rate the following attributes on a scale of 1 to 4, with 4 being the highest.

	Points
Phone manners	_____
Understandability	_____
Confidence	_____
Word pictures	_____
Sales effectiveness	_____
Sensitivity to others	_____
Positive attitude	_____
Voice quality	_____
Acceptable accent	_____
Comfort level on call	_____
Ability to listen	_____
Speech rate	_____
Contagious enthusiasm	_____
Ability to do job	_____
Total	_____

Would I have hired this person today based on my first impression?
Circle answer:

Yes   No   Maybe

gram called "Managing for Success" from TTI Software, Ltd. There are several versions: one for field salespeople, another for managers, and a "Telesales Coach Version." Let me briefly describe how the program works.

It was created and developed by Bill Bonnstetter based on the work of Dr. William M. Martson and his book, *The Emotions of Normal People*. He reduces human behavior to four basic characteristics:

1. **Dominance**—the drive to overcome opposing forces of perceived inferior strength to the self.

2. **Inducement**—the attempt to ally forces to the self through persuasive means.

3. **Submission**—the acquiescence of the self to a perceived allied force.

4. **Compliance**—the subordination of the self to a hostile force of superior strength.

Martson believed human beings begin life full of the dominance-type behavior. As infants, we expect our cries and tantrums to produce the results we want. As time passes, the dominance response is modified and the other behaviors arise.

Children who are always allowed to have their way, whose parents always give in, retain a large amount of dominance in adulthood. Children whose parents gently steer them away from what they want to what the parents want for them develop submission behavior. Martson used the word "submission" as a scientific term, meaning the response that occurs when we willingly give up what we initially thought we wanted in favor of behavior desired by our parents, because we have been persuaded (or led through affection and positive reinforcement to feel) that what our parents want may be best for us, too.

The compliance response arises when the demands of children are modified through less positive means. When we are forced to modify our behavior under threat of punishment, for example, the response is classified as compliance rather than submission. According to Martson, the learning of submission is pleasant; the learning of compliance is unpleasant. We submit because we want to submit. We comply because we are forced to.

Except in those rare cases when demands are always met—or, to put it another way, the children are "spoiled rotten"—all children learn to modify their behavior by either willingly submitting to or reluctantly complying with the wishes of their parents.

Inducement is the type of behavior by which we attempt to get what we want by persuading rather than demanding. Babies do not know how to persuade; they merely demand. As children mature, they learn that persuasion is often more effective than demanding. The more success children have at talking their parents into things, the more inducement behavior they will retain as adults.

According to Martson, I is to S as C is to D. In other words, the gentle persuasion of inducement brings about the pleasant submission response. The demanding dominance behavior brings about the compliance response. I-style parenting causes an increase in S behavior, and D-style parenting causes a rise in C behavior.

Martson found that definite characteristics or traits could be ascribed to each style of behavior.

Characteristics	*Behavior*
D Style	Aggressive, demanding, forceful
I Style	Verbally persuasive, optimistic, trusting
S Style	Calm, amiable, relaxed
C Style	Perfectionist, accurate, fearful

As you might guess, much depends on the degree to which each of these characteristics is present.

The program only takes 10-15 minutes to run. Each candidate is asked to rate groups of words as they apply to themselves. Once this is completed, a report is generated. The report describes the candidates' positive and negative attributes in light of telephone sales.

The type of person you want depends on the type of telemarketing you're doing. For example, for outbound sales work, you want high "D" and "I" scores. Inbound would call for more "S" and "C." The perfect telemarketer has some of all the basic characteristics, but you'll learn through experience what personality combination works best for your operation. To me, the value of running the tests is establishing a baseline for comparison of candidates.

Handling the Compensation Issue

You will never get through even the first interview without discussing compensation. As with any sales job, this should consist of a combination of salary and incentives.

The salary is the TSR's base wage. In most cases, it varies between the minimum wage and $8 per hour, depending on location, industry practice, the product being sold, company policy, educational requirements, etc. Some unusual situations may call for graduate engineers or chemists as TSRs. These positions usually offer salaries slightly below those offered for entry-level salespeople in these fields.

The TSR incentive is the other part of the total wage package; it should allow TSRs to increase their base earnings by 25 to 50 percent. The incentive should be kept flexible and should be paid often—at least monthly; better yet, weekly or even daily. For example, in one month you can put on an intensive push for new accounts and pay the TSRs a handsome bounty on each one they capture. In the following month, incentive compensation can be tied to reactivating dormant accounts. Or you might want TSRs to

---

Exhibit 4–2

Sample Job Description

Telephone Sales Representative

OBJECTIVE: To sell and service the company's current customers and to help convert prospects for our products to new customers.

DUTIES:

1. Place and receive telephone calls to and from customers and prospects. No fewer than four or more than six hours per day on the phone.
2. Sell the company's products and services on each call.
3. Solve customer problems and remove obstacles blocking further sales.
4. Keep track of and report daily telephone selling activities to the supervisor:
   A. Total number of dialings per day
   B. Number of sales presentations or conversations with decision makers each day
   C. Number and dollar volume of orders taken each day
   D. Number of daily callbacks, disconnects, no answers, and busies
   E. Amount of time spent on the phone selling as opposed to paperwork, problem solving, training, and looking up phone numbers
5. Attend training sessions.
6. Review call reports with supervisor.
7. Study and improve telemarketing skills.
8. Provide customers with the kind of high-quality service that builds loyalty.
9. Actively seek and pursue new customers.

---

generate new leads for the field sales force. Don't tie the incentive to a single criterion; innovate and make it work for your company in a variety of ways. It is the one area where you can easily create excitement and focus on short-term goals.

The average TSR earns approximately $15,000 per year based on a 40-hour work week involving about 30 hours of calling. Six hours a day, five days a week is the maximum a TSR should be on the phone if it is intensive. Additional time is spent on paperwork.

One last thought: in most major metropolitan centers, you now have access to telemarketing temporary employment agencies. These should be considered for seasonal or special telemarketing promotions that are intense but of short duration.

I have also been very successful in hiring part-time TSRs from the local college student population and retired or semiretired individuals. I've had several very competent, long-term telephone saleswomen who want something to supplement Social Security. Don't overlook this segment of the work force.

5

Planning for Higher Telemarketing Productivity: Tracking and Measuring Telemarketing Results

An understanding of how telemarketing activity and productivity are related and measured is a prerequisite to operating a profitable telemarketing center and determining TSR workloads and/or quotas. This can be obtained by monitoring and analyzing the calling activity of the telemarketing center. As you develop your tracking methodology, keep this old adage in mind: "What gets measured gets done!"

Most telemarketers measure their telemarketing performance for a given period of time on a per-hour or per-TSR basis. Depending on the product being offered and the goals of a particular campaign, this may be calculated in several different ways, including the number of orders per hour, dollar sales per hour, or appointments or surveys per hour. The measure of time can be either the TSR's total hours worked or just his or her actual calling hours. Total hours worked reflects total costs more accurately and, therefore, is preferred.

As a rule of thumb, if the product or service being telemarketed is priced at less than $100, you can conservatively estimate an average of one to four orders per hour worked per TSR. For products priced at over $100, budget one-half to three orders per hour per TSR. This rule of thumb provides a quick and convenient method of converting TSR calling hours into unit and dollar sales estimates. More detailed and accurate approaches are described below.

Break-Even Analysis

Another important element is establishing the hourly sales required to break even. That is the amount of sales per hour needed to cover all the costs associated with a particular telemarketing campaign, department, or product. The break-even figure is calculated by dividing all the costs related to operating the telemarketing center by the gross contribution to overhead of product sold, then dividing this figure by the total number of hours charged to the project. Some managers prefer a per-unit standard.

The break-even calculation shows the rate of sales per hour the center has to make to cover all the costs. Any sales over the break-even level contribute directly to profits.

For example, if we assume that a product sells for $100 and has a total of $60 in variable costs (unit cost of goods sold, fulfillment, long-distance call charges, TSR incentives, and so on), the gross profit would be $40 per unit sold. If the center's fixed costs (TSR salaries and benefits, rent, utilities, telephone service, equipment, management, etc.) for the five-week period planned for the telemarketing campaign totaled $12,000, we would have to sell 300 units ($12,000 divided by $40) to break even on the campaign.

Further, if the center had two TSRs calling six hours a day for the duration of the campaign, the total calling time would be 300 hours (2 TSRs × 6 hours/day × 5 days/week × 5 weeks). The hourly break-even would be one unit per hour (300 units divided by 300 hours). This means the center in our example would have to sell, on average, one unit of the product per calling hour for the campaign to break even.

Using this simple model in the early planning stages of a campaign helps you assess the feasibility of the effort and identify any economies of scale. For instance, it shows the bottom-line effect of increasing the price of the product, the number of TSRs, or the number of calls completed per hour. You spend your resources, be they incentives to your TSRs or automating your center, where they make the most impact on reaching your goals.

Future Value of a Customer

Evaluating a campaign on the basis of its per-hour results makes good short-term economic sense. But the longer-term economics of the future value of a new customer also deserve consideration. Future value is represented by an estimate of the total sales anticipated from a new customer over the course of his or her buying lifetime.

For example, the prior sales history of a newsletter publisher shows that a subscriber, once acquired, renews his or her subscription an average of three times. And in any given five-year period, the average subscriber also attends at least one seminar and buys one book. Additionally, 50 percent of first-time newsletter subscribers subscribe to a second newsletter. By projecting the stream of income from all these revenue sources over the buying life of a typical new subscriber, the publisher develops more realistic guidelines for determining how much can be spent to obtain each new subscriber. This figure is much higher than if the publisher based subscriber acquisition costs solely on the income received from the initial sale.

The break-even should always be calculated in the way that makes the most sense over the buying life cycle of a typical customer. Unless the product/service is a one-time-only sale, limiting the measurement (or evaluation) of the telemarketing performance to the first sale does not make economic sense.

Tracking Campaign Results

Like any worthwhile marketing effort, successful telemarketing takes time. Growth and improvement are incremental and require constant testing and fine-tuning. You should always be prepared to refine the tracking and evaluation methods as conditions in the marketplace shift, as new sales patterns emerge, and as new selling approaches and strategies are tested and validated.

Putting together a tracking system that will help you plan tomorrow's activities *and* measure today's results is extremely important. It requires the creation of an ongoing historical record of telemarketing activity that becomes a valuable planning tool for measuring current performance and making informed decisions. It also enables you to establish sales quotas against which exceptional TSR performance can be measured and rewarded—an important duty of management.

The Key to a Successful Tracking System

If you decide to use an automated call system, it can do much of the necessary tracking. Nevertheless, you may want to study the following to get a feel for the type of numbers you'll want to review daily. Let's begin with one of the most basic report forms, the TSR's Daily Telephone Activity Log (see Figure 5–1).

The purpose of the Daily Telephone Activity Log is to provide a simple and efficient method of keeping tabs on how each TSR is using his or her time. The information to be gleaned from this form is invaluable and provides the basis for many of the decisions

FIGURE 5–1

Daily Telephone Activity Log

Name __Phyllis__   Date _____

Station __272__

① Time in __8:30__ Out __12:00__ In __12:30__ Out __5:00__ Hours Worked __8__

Breakdown:

	Time (hours)	Percentage
② Review/Training	.25	3
③ Paper Work/Problem Solving	1.25	16
④ Break/Meals	.50	6
⑤ Look Ups	—	—
⑥ Calling	6.00	75

DIALINGS

	⑦Look Ups	⑧Completed Calls		⑨Call Backs	⑩Busies	⑪Dis-Connects	⑫No Answers	
		Sales TH TH. II	12	TH.TH. TH.TH. TH.TH. II	TH TH TH. TH	TH TH TH	TH. TH	T O T A L
		"Maybe's" IIII	4					
		"No's" TH.TH. TH.TH.	20					
Totals	0			36	32	22	20	10	120
Percentages	0			30%	27%	18%	17%	8%	100%

Closing/Orders/Appointments/Etc.

		Sales	
		$Volume	Units
Handbook of Toxic Waste ⑬ Product #1	$188 each	$2,256	12
Product #2			
Product #3			
Product #4			
Product #5			
⑭TOTALS		$2,256	12

⑮ Ratio: Total $ __2,256__ sold / __8__ hours = $ __282__ per hour

⑯ Number of Leads/Accounts __135__ less "Nos" __66__ = __69__ actives.

that must be made to assure the success of the operation. It will help you to refer to the sample form often during the discussions that follow.

TSR TIME ALLOCATIONS

Entry 1 on the form covers the TSR's arrival and departure times, including the meal break, and shows the total hours worked for the day. Entries 2 to 6 divide the day's total hours into "Review/ Training," "Paperwork/Problem Solving," "Breaks/Meals," "Look-ups" (looking up phone numbers on lists that do not include them or numbers that are illegible or incorrect), and "Calling." These entries have been converted to the nearest quarter-hour. To the right of the time column is another column showing the time spent on each activity as a percentage of the total hours worked for the day. These numbers are crucial in the manager's daily review, because he or she must determine the precise percentage of time each TSR spends actually calling. That's when the results are achieved!

Generally, the percentage of time spent calling should be in the 70–80 percent range for an eight-hour workday and close to 100 percent for a six-hour workday. Allowances must be made, of course, for a new TSR, or for a product that requires an unusual amount of paperwork following each order.

A rigorously maintained time log might reveal inefficient time allocations. A TSR who spends 25 percent or more of the workday solving problems or doing paperwork cannot effectively telemarket. This is a situation requiring adjustment. Look-ups that require 10 percent or more of the workday indicate a list problem requiring investigation.

Entry 1 on the log shows that on April 3, Phyllis, the TSR in this example, worked an eight-hour shift, from 8:30 a.m. to 5:00 p.m., with a half-hour for lunch. Her task is to call the supervisors of engineering departments of major manufacturers to find out if their plants produce toxic waste and, if so, who in the organization is responsible for its disposal. Once she locates the right person, she attempts to sell her firm's product, *The Handbook of Toxic Waste*, which costs $188 and offers quarterly updates to help customers stay in compliance with Environmental Protection Agency and state regulations.

Phyllis's activity log shows that she spends 15 minutes preparing for the day's calls (Entry 2), one hour and 15 minutes doing paperwork (Entry 3), a total of 30 minutes on breaks (Entry 4), no look-up time (Entry 5) and a total of six hours making calls (Entry 6). Paperwork/problem solving takes up 16 percent of Phyllis's time. This entails writing orders and filling requests for literature, as well as typing labels and writing notes to people who show interest in the *Handbook* but do not buy on the first call. The informational packets used for follow-up mailing are stuffed by the printer and ready to mail. Phyllis also has special stationery with her name on it for this purpose. The last hour of the day is set aside for this work, filing, and other loose ends.

Before she begins each day's calls, Phyllis spends 15 minutes reviewing the *Handbook's* most recent quarterly update for articles of particular importance. These become part of her script.

Dialing Results

Now we will review her dialings for the day (entries 7 through 12 in the Daily Telephone Activity Log, Figure 5-1).

Since Phyllis had no look-ups on this day, we can conclude that the list she is using is of good quality, at least from the standpoint of phone numbers. The next activity is "Completed Calls" (Entry 8). In telemarketing parlance, "completed calls" has a special meaning. It is a call during which the TSR talks to the decision maker and delivers the sales message. For example, if Phyllis connects with a vice president of engineering and finds that he or she is not the person at the company responsible for toxic waste disposal, she will ask to be transferred to the person who is. If she finds that person unavailable, the dialing is recorded not as a completed call but as a "callback" (Entry 9). A callback is a call during which the TSR reached the proper office but not the decision maker and must make subsequent calls to talk to the prospect.

"Busies" (Entry 10), "Disconnects" (Entry 11), and "No Answers" (Entry 12) are self-explanatory. They should be monitored closely by the telemarketing manager, since they may indicate an inefficient list. They may also help to identify unproductive times of day.

Note that there is space for a "line stroke" tally for each call made by Phyllis. The TSRs are trained to record each and every dialing with a line stroke in the appropriate box immediately after it is completed.

If there are disproportionate numbers of callbacks, no answers, or busies, the TSRs may be calling at the wrong time of the day for your particular prospects. There are times during which certain types of people are more or less inaccessible, as the following list shows. You should develop similar guidelines for your customers or prospects.

1. *Stock and commodity brokers* watch the markets and talk with clients from 7:00 a.m. to 3:15 p.m. Calling after 3:00 p.m. results in a better connect rate.

2. *Grade school or high school teachers*—after 4:00 p.m. or in the evenings at home.

3. *Physicians*—early in the morning, 7:30 a.m. to 10:00 p.m., or after 4:00 p.m.

4. *Lawyers*—before 11:00 a.m. and after 2:00 p.m.

5. *Engineers*—varies by professional specialty. Civil engineers are usually available early in the morning and late in the afternoon. At other times they may be out on construction

jobs. In the northern part of the country, they are nearly impossible to reach in the late fall because of their rush to finish jobs before the frost hits.

6. *Bankers*—available from late morning and through lunch until early afternoon.

7. *Newspaper people*—if they work for a morning paper, early afternoon; if for an evening paper, early evening at home.

8. *Purchasing agents*—first thing in the morning, but not on Mondays and Fridays.

9. *Executives*—much depends on their area of responsibility, but in general, Monday mornings and Friday afternoons are unproductive telemarketing times. Sales and marketing executives travel a lot, so plan extra callbacks.

Learning your prospects'/customers' working and leisure habits pays off. Calling only to find them unavailable just wastes time and money and can be avoided. Worst of all, it discourages your TSRs.

Frequent disconnects—anything over 15 percent is considered abnormally high—usually indicate a bad list. If a rented list has bad phone numbers, you may be able to recover some of the rental cost by selling them back to the list owner. A reputable list owner wants them and pays for them. If an in-house list causes problems, seek the origin of the errors. Compare samples of the original input data with the list entries the TSRs are given to work. You may find a problem in your data entry procedure.

Returning to the results in the sample activity log, we find Phyllis makes 36 completed calls (30 percent of her 120 total dialings for the day) resulting in 12 sales, 4 "maybes," and 20 definite "no's." She has 32 callbacks (27 percent), 22 busies (18 percent), and 20 disconnects (17 percent). Phyllis also has 10 no-answers (8 percent), somewhat high for a list of manufacturing firms or any business normally open during regular hours. A good telemarketing manager would recognize this and begin searching for a new list source.

Further analysis of the completed calls section of Phyllis's activity log shows that she makes 20 dialings per hour on average (120 total calls divided by 6 hours). This is a very satisfactory rate for an operation that does not use automated dialing equipment.

Dialings per hour can range from as few as 5 to as many as 40. Although dialings per hour is a legitimate measure of efficiency, its suitability depends on many factors that must be taken into account before a standard for a telemarketing center can be established. For example, a low rate of dialings per hour—say, less than 15—can result when TSRs are inundated with paperwork. Constant paperwork interrupts a TSR's rhythm, and when the flow of calls is too frequently broken, the quality and spontaneity of the calls degenerates. And, more important, so do sales per hour.

Sloppy lists also reduce productivity. If TSRs must rely on lead sheets or warranty cards that are filled out in longhand, they may have problems reading the names and numbers. Frustration inevitably ensues and dialings per hour decline. The frustration eventually shows in their voice and sales decline.

TSRs should be provided with some administrative time each week to clean their lists, if necessary. First, they should sort out the names or numbers that cannot be read or that have phone numbers missing. These should be put aside while the TSRs call the other names on the list. If the list proves to be hot, you will have no problem getting the TSRs to investigate and pursue the incomplete or inaccurate names. If it is cold, there is no need to bother with it further. Time and money are saved.

Very high dialing rates—40 or more per hour—can be achieved by using computerized telemarketing workstations. The computer automatically dials each number and lets it ring a predetermined number of times (6 to 10 rings). If there is no answer, a wrong number, or a disconnect, the TSR hits a key, the problem is recorded by the computer, and the next number is automatically dialed. No-answers are immediately stored in a callback file. In such a system, the paperwork required of the TSR at the end of a successful call is reduced to a keystroke or two to record what transpired.

For planning and budgeting purposes in a nonautomated center, a dialings-per-hour rate of 15 can be assumed if the list is legible and accurate. Use this as a guide to measure how long it will take to get through a list and/or how many TSRs are needed. For instance, it takes approximately 67 hours to complete 1,000 initial dialings at a rate of 15 per hour. This would be more than two weeks of calling for a single TSR (assuming six calling hours per day and a five-day work week), or about one week for two TSRs.

Don't forget, on average a TSR would reach about 25 to 50 percent of the names on the list on the first attempted call. This would result in between 250 and 500 callbacks on the 1,000-name list, or 16 to 32 hours of additional calling for a second attempt. Therefore, after adjusting for callbacks, the 1,000-name list requires about three weeks for one TSR, or one and a half weeks for two. Additionally, you might want to make several attempts at hard-to-reach prospects.

TSRs need guidelines on how many times they should dial each number. Should they try every name on the list just once? Twice? Thrice? Four times? In most cases this depends on the list or the type of customer being solicited. It also may depend on the size of the list. If you have a relatively unlimited universe of names, try two or three calls. With small lists, try six or seven. In any case, always try at least twice, with the calls at different times of the day.

Entry 13 on the Daily Telephone Activity Log summarizes the number of closings, orders, or appointments that were achieved by the TSR for each product being offered that day. Both unit and dollar volume results are shown. Phyllis had only one product to sell (*The Handbook of Toxic Waste*). She sold 12 units for total sales of $2,256.

Most telemarketing managers inevitably focus first on entries 14 and 15 of the Daily Log, which show total unit and dollar sales per hour worked per day. Our example shows that April 3 was a productive day for Phyllis. Her 12 sales, totaling $2,256, resulted in $282 in sales per hour worked. Keep in mind that this is not the final sales tally, because it does not take into account how many units may be returned by customers and how many of them will be "no pays." Nevertheless, this is pretty good—a break-even analysis of the campaign showed that it costs only $25 to $30 an hour to operate Phyllis' workstation.

Entry 16 of the Daily Log indicates to the telemarketing manager that Phyllis needs additional leads. Of the 135 total leads she had at the start of the day, she used 66 and has only 79 remaining. A lead is considered "used" or "dead" when the dialing results in a "completed call," a "disconnect," or a "no" after two or three unsuccessful attempts.

Summarizing a Center's Daily Activity

If a center has more than one TSR, an additional activity report is needed to compile the individual Daily Telephone Activity logs of all the TSRs. This form is referred to as the Summary of Daily Telephone Activity Logs.

The Summary should be completed as often as the activities of the center demand—at least monthly or, preferably, weekly. These, in turn, can be combined to provide quarterly, semiannual, or annual summaries. At the outset of a new campaign, it makes sense to compile a Daily Summary until the direction of the campaign becomes clear.

In our example, we assumed that there are four other TSRs in the center besides Phyllis, and that two perform 20 percent below her April 3 performance and two 10 percent above. The Weekly Summary for the week ending April 4 is shown in Figure 5-2. Note that it follows the format of the Daily Log, thereby making it easy to compile the data and analyze the results.

Many centers use personal computers and a spreadsheet program to make an overlay of the activity log. This allows the manager to play "What if?" games with the data, such as "What happens to a campaign's bottom line if dialings increase by 10 percent?" This capability can provide the telemarketing manager with valuable insights into how best to increase productivity.

The analysis of the Daily Telephone Activity Log also applies to the Summary and need not be repeated.

ANALYZING RESULTS

Data from the Summary Logs can be used to compare the performance of each TSR against the combined performance of the group. The TSRs that lag behind group averages would be encouraged to improve, and the most productive might be given additional incentives or rewards.

A center's activity and its performance goals can be graphed using data from the Summary Logs. Figure 5-3 is a graph based on our example. It tracks the center's dialings per hour, completed calls per hour, and sales per hour for the first four months of the year. It also includes a break-even line at 0.25 sales per hour.

In the example, the estimated fixed cost per calling hour for the center was $30. The *Handbook* is priced at $188. If we assume that the cost of goods sold, fulfillment, and other direct costs for each *Handbook* sold total $68, then the gross profit of each one would be $120. This would put the break-even point at 0.25 sales per hour ($30 divided by $120) or two sales per eight-hour day ($30 × 8 hours = $240 divided by $120 = 2 sales). Taking into account anticipated returns and nonpayments, the break-even point would be somewhat higher. In this example, it might increase break-even to three sales per day.

FIGURE 5–2

Summary of Daily Telephone Activity Logs

_____Week ending April 4_____
(Weekly, Monthly, Quarterly, Annual)

Date _____   Div./Dept. __TM Center_____

Time Useage Breakdown:	Hours	Percentage
① Training/Review	6.25	3%
② Paper work/Problem Solving	31.25	16%
③ Breaks/Meals	12.50	6%
④ Look ups (phone numbers)	—	—
⑤ Calling	150.00	75%
⑥ TOTALS	200.00	100%

⑦ Total Number of Telemarketers: · 5

⑧ Average hours per week per telemarketer 40

⑨ Average hours per day per telemarketer 8

CALL SUMMARY

Completed Calls: Number (%)

⑩ Sales
(Orders, Appt's, etc) 330 (33%)

	Number (%)	Numbers	Percentages
⑪ Maybe	110 (11%)		
⑫ Dead Leads	560 (56%)		
⑬ TOTAL Completed Calls		1000	30%
⑭ Call backs		890	27%
⑮ Busy		615	18%
⑯ Disconnects.......................		560	17%
⑰ No answers.......................		280	8%
⑱ TOTAL DIALINGS		3,345	100%

⑲ Dialings per hour worked: (Entry ⑱ ÷ Entry ⑥) 16.7

⑳ Completed calls per hr. worked: (Entry ⑬ ÷ Entry ⑥) 5

㉑ Total sales (Units/orders) 330/$62,040.00

㉒ Sales (Units/$ orders) per hour
worked (Entry ㉑ ÷ Entry ⑥) 1.65/$310.20

LEAD/ACCOUNT TALLY

㉓ Total leads/accounts available at beginning of period 5.000

㉔ New leads/accounts acquired .... ADD —

㉕ Dead leads/accounts lost .... LESS 1,840

㉖ TOTAL leads/accounts at end of period 3,160

㉗ Leads/Accounts per Telemarketer 632

㉘ Is action required at this time to obtain new or more
leads/accounts?   [X]Yes   [ ] No

FIGURE 5–3

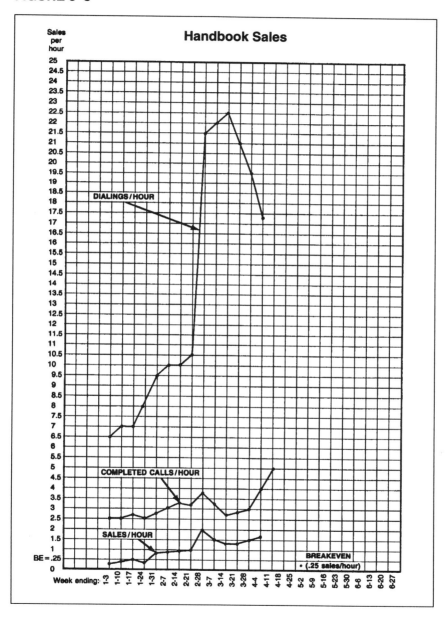

A close look at Figure 5–3 shows a dramatic rise in dialings per hour with a simultaneous decline in sales and completed calls during the weeks of March 14 and 21. This may indicate list problems—accumulating an unusually high number of "disconnects," which are quick, unproductive calls.

Summary

This chapter presented the basic methods of planning, monitoring, and evaluating the performance of a telephone marketing effort. Your methods, of course, can become much more sophisticated. For instance, there are advanced, computerized telephone systems that record and analyze every dialing made during a specific campaign and apply the phone charges, as well as other costs incurred. This level of precision was once available only to the very large telemarketing centers. But the widespread use of personal computers and the development of hundreds of software programs for marketing, sales, and telemarketing have changed all that, as we'll discuss when we get to automating your center.

Planning the Telemarketing Facilities: Space and Equipment

6

An important but often overlooked factor in planning a successful telemarketing center is the configuration of equipment and space: where and how are the TSRs going to be situated? What special kinds of furniture and equipment will they need?

Workstation Requirements

The proper amount of space required for a telemarketing center depends on how many TSRs will be hired and on how the noise of the center is to be controlled. A typical module for a four-TSR workstation is illustrated in Figure 6–1.

In this configuration, the four TSRs can be comfortably officed in 100 square feet of space. Such workstations feature built-in filing drawers, cork panels to reduce noise levels, and raceway for electrical cords. One can be installed easily in a 15' by 15' room.

FIGURE 6–1

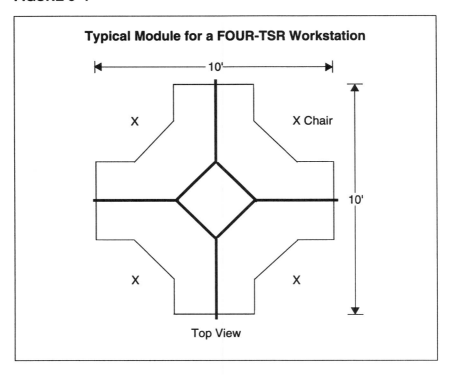

Other designs are available which install laterally—along a wall, for example (see Figure 6–2). Such stations would be approximately five feet in length and depth and would accommodate a single TSR. Four TSRs would require 100 square feet (4 TSRs × 5' long × 5' deep).

If workstations prove too elaborate for the center's budget, a secretarial desk or table of some sort with easy access to a file cabinet will suffice. The size and sophistication of the furniture is not what's important. The overriding consideration is to provide TSRs with the space and equipment necessary for effective performance. For budgeting purposes, most centers plan on at least 50 square feet for each TSR, including space for aisles.

FIGURE 6–2

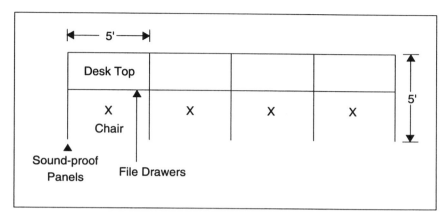

CHAIRS AND HEADSETS

Two pieces of equipment in a telemarketing center demand special consideration. The first is the TSR's chair. It must be a good one; the TSR will be in it most of the workday. Experience has shown that the quality of the chair directly influences the TSR's attitude and behavior toward customers and prospects. Choosing a chair seems a simple enough decision, but it is crucial. Not all TSRs are physically the same, so more than one style is often required. Talk with a competent office furniture supplier.

Telephone headsets represent the second important purchase. Headsets enable TSRs to use their hands to take notes, search for price lists, take orders, and so on. In addition, many people "talk" with their hands. Their gesturing adds inflection and excitement to their voices, which, of course, improves the quality of their calls. Headsets also are more comfortable to use over extended periods of time than hand-held receivers. In addition, they tend to discourage interruptions by others in the room, because fellow workers are never sure when their neighbor is online. A wide variety of styles is available. If practical, let your TSRs choose their own.

The TeleEasel

It is very important to organize all the materials the TSRs need at their fingertips when calling. A freestanding easel was developed to accomplish this task (see Figure 6-3). It is called, quite aptly, the TeleEasel. The ones I use are fabricated by a local plexiglass distributor for about $25 each.

FIGURE 6–3

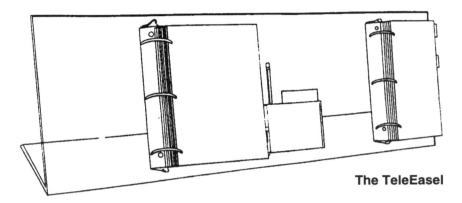

The TeleEasel

The TeleEasel has two three-ring holders permanently attached to it. The binder on the left, as you face it, accepts standard 8½" × 11" pages. Sales literature, pricing sheets, sample forms, specification pages, service bulletins, parts lists, exploded drawings, sales territory maps, and such are placed on this side.

The three-ring holder on the right takes 6" × 11" materials. This is for TSR reference materials, such as scripts, lists of benefits, lists of common objections with the appropriate responses, and so on. All these materials together are commonly referred to as the telemarketing reference guide (discussed in detail in Chapter 10). The 6-inch width is designed to make it easier for the TSRs to read. We type the scripts, etc., on plain paper, copy them onto heavier paper stock, and three-hole punch them for mounting on the TeleEasel.

A common substitute is a sales presentation binder with a built-in easel. Tabletop podiums can also be employed for this purpose. There are even wall-mounted versions commercially available if desk or countertop space is at a premium. Each of these devices serves to place all the information your TSRs require right at their fingertips. If they constantly have to interrupt or break off calls to search for information, they'll lose the attention of their listeners and their credibility.

Phone Service and Equipment

Phone service and equipment are pivotal to the proper functioning of a telemarketing center. This has never been truer than since the breakup of AT&T, which has resulted in a proliferation of telephone services, the portability of toll-free numbers, more equipment manufacturers, and a variety of long-distance services— AT&T, MCI, ITT, TMI, SPRINT, resellers, and many others.

SOME HINTS ON SELECTING PHONE SERVICE

Before contracting for any phone service, thoroughly investigate the following:

- **Quality of the Lines:** Poor line quality results in lost sales. No supplier, of course, ever admits to poor line quality, so test the lines extensively before allowing installation. Demand loud, clean connections. Consult with other customers of the carriers being considered.

- **Dialing Time:** How many digits must be dialed to complete a long-distance call? Some long-distance services require a six- or eight-digit code in addition to the area code and number. Find out if, and at what cost, speed dialing is available. A long access code can be maddening to a TSR expected to make 30 dialings per hour over a six-hour shift.

With the advent of equal access and increased competition, this has become less of a concern.

- **Recordkeeping:** Ask for billing information and samples of a typical monthly report provided by the carriers. These should provide enough data on each extension to enable the telemarketing manager to estimate telephone costs and evaluate individual TSR performance.

- **Billing Methods:** In order to control costs, you will need to know when billing for a call begins. ITT begins billing after eight rings; others wait 45 or 77 seconds; others do not begin until the phone is answered.

Does the carrier charge a start-up fee when you first come online? Are there installation costs? Volume discounts? Surcharges for credit card calls? Higher rates for off-net calls? An estimate of your regular monthly bill, including all of the services and options you expect to use, is needed to compare prospective carriers.

- **Inbound Toll-Free Lines:** Are you planning to have toll-free inbound service? If you are, determine whether this service is available from the carrier being considered. If so, at what cost? Chapter 12 addresses telemarketing centers that have inbound calls as their primary function.

TELEPHONE EQUIPMENT CONSIDERATIONS AND OPTIONS

Headsets, as suggested earlier, are very important. There is, moreover, an enormous array of options available to further customize any phone system to meet the specific needs of a given telemarketing center. The list below, though hardly comprehensive, suggests the range of possibilities.

- **Speed Dialing Devices:** Very useful if TSRs call the same number repeatedly. The more advanced phone systems usually include this feature as standard.

- **Numeric Display:** Shows the outgoing number being dialed. Digital displays of numbers being dialed improve dialing accuracy. Separate phone lines or extensions can be assigned to different product lines or corporate divisions, so that when a call comes in, the operator can easily identify the line or extension displayed and respond to the call appropriately.

- **Conferencing, Monitoring, or Three-Way Calling:** In smaller centers, the manager can use the relatively inexpensive conference or three-way calling feature to coach TSRs. Larger centers usually opt for more expensive and sophisticated observation and silent monitoring systems.

- **Automatic Callback:** This can be a timesaver, especially if TSRs can determine when the callback will take place. (In many cases, however, it is at the customer's or prospect's convenience.)

- **Barge-In Feature or Off-Hook Signaling:** Managers can use these signals to contact TSRs who are on calls.

- **Do Not Disturb or Busy-Out and Free-Station Search:** The do not disturb and busy-out features are useful when TSRs have paperwork to complete or are on break. The free-station search feature, which locates a free TSR when all the other lines are busy, is a very useful tool. Another worthwhile option is the automatic hold, with an interesting message or music for the waiting party. Studies indicate that people who are entertained while on hold wait longer and complain less about the wait.

- **Message Handling:** Messages can be handled manually ("While You Were Out" slips) or electronically with such devices as paging, a message light on the phones, a single-line message display on the phones, beepers, answering machines, call forwarding, answering services or pools, station search feature, electronic mail, etc.

- **Recordkeeping:** Recordkeeping options include automatic summaries of all calls made by location and time, detailed records of each call made, and daily estimates of phone charges—all identified by phone extension or individual TSR.

- **Call Distribution:** This should be considered only by telemarketing centers making an extremely high volume of calls. The wide array of automatic call distribution equipment available can be programmed according to the requirements of your center and can substantially reduce online costs.

The more features a system has, the more expensive it will be. Therefore, it is important to evaluate, through cost/benefit analysis, the gains resulting from each option. If a phone feature such as station search increases sales significantly by routing incoming orders to open TSRs fast, it may well be worth the additional expense.

TELEPHONE SWITCHING CONTROL

Another important decision is the location of the switching control device. Basically, there are four alternatives:

1. **Terminal-Based:** All of the various system functions and options are built into each individual telephone station. This can be cost-effective for small telemarketing centers but becomes more expensive as the center grows. This may be the best system for centers that never expect to have more than five TSRs on the phones, although it may somewhat limit the number of other options.

2. **Central-Based:** Commonly known as private branch exchange (PBX) systems, these are designed for medium to large centers. All the functions are built into a master switch-

ing device and down-loaded to the individual stations. These systems can have enormous capacity, handling hundreds of phones, and may require a central receptionist or operator.

3. **Remote-Based:** The master switching device is located at the local phone company's facilities. If dependability is your number-one priority, this might be the best approach. The local phone company, with all its capabilities, provides an immediate backup system if problems occur.

4. **Hybrid-Based:** A system in which some features are built into the individual telephone sets while others, such as call forwarding, are handled by the local phone company.

A checklist has been prepared to help you select the telephone system best suited to your center's activity. (See Exhibit 6–1.)

AUTOMATIC CALL DISTRIBUTION

Automatic Call Distributors (ACD) are computerized devices that quickly process a large number of incoming or outgoing calls. They can manage up to several hundred phones simultaneously and become cost-efficient when 10 to 15 lines are in heavy use (5 to 10 online hours per day). When shopping for an ACD, consider these factors:

- **Line Maximizing:** Most long-distance services offer volume discounts. If the ACD has the capability to make optimum use of the lines available to the system and can run up the most hours on the least number of lines, it may pay for itself quickly in volume discounts.

- **Call Accounting:** Call reports should be on a station-by-station basis and should include area code, time of call, length of call, number of calls per station, trunk line usage, etc.—all with daily averages for each. These are just some of

Exhibit 6–1

Telephone System Options Checklist

Rate each option according to its importance to your particular business, using this scale:

  9 = very important
  5 = somewhat important
  1 = not important at all

I. **Message Handling Options**
    A. Manual system
    B. Paging
        1. Intercom
        2. Remote portable device
        3. Message waiting light
        4. Alpha numeric display
    C. Answering machine
    D. Voice mail
    E. Electronic mail
    F. Call forwarding
    G. Night transfer
    H. Call waiting
    I. Station hunting
    J. Answering pool
    K. Automatic attendant

II. **Traffic Pattern Options**
    A. Internal station-to-station dialing
    B. Direct inward dialing
    C. Direct outward dialing
    D. Automatic call distributor

III. **Tracking/Billing/Cost Control Options**
    A. Internal calls only allowed
    B. Toll area restrictions
    C. Least-cost routing system
    D. Station message detail recording
    E. Customer dialed accounting recording

Exhibit 6–1 (continued)

IV. **Privacy and Security Options**

    A.   Privacy protection

    B.   Safety devices interconnect

        1.   Fire/Smoke

        2.   Temperature

        3.   Tampering

        4.   Automatic door phones

V. **Efficiency/Convenience Options**

    A.   Speed dialing

    B.   Numeric display

    C.   Conference or 3-way calling

    D.   Hands-free answer back

    E.   Automatic callback (repeat dialing)

    F.   Last number redial

    G.   Off-hook signaling

    H.   Flexible ringing pattern (distinctive rings)

    I.   Barge-in feature

    J.   Do not disturb

    K.   Monitoring or call observation

VI. **Nonvoice Capacity Options**

    A.   Local area networking (LAN)

    B.   Simultaneous voice/data transmission lines

    C.   Line splitters

    D.   Touchtone terminals

    E.   Digital switching and transmission

VII. **Image**

    A.   Equipment style

    B.   State-of-the-art options

VIII. **Types of Switching Systems**

    A.   Terminal-based

    B.   Central control device (switch, PBX, PABX)

    C.   Remote-based device (CENTREX)

    D.   Hybrid

the data included. Determine whether the system's record-keeping software can be customized to your specific needs, now and in the future.

- **Call Distribution:** How are the calls distributed to the TSRs? This can be very important if the TSRs are on commission. Can this feature be programmed to meet your needs?

- **Queuing Options:** Do the options offered match the needs of the center? How long is a call held? Can a prerecorded message or music be played while the calling party is on hold? How easy is it to change the message or make other adjustments? Can calls be camped online?

- **Flexibility in Routing:** An ACD can be set up to route various kinds of incoming calls to appropriate stations, where they will be answered promptly and expeditiously. For instance, you might wish to separate service from sales calls. Also find out how easy would it be to change the routes.

- **Efficiency Features:** Some ACDs automatically connect to an open station without the TSR having to press the "Answer" button. Or the ACD can be programmed to open the station up to a new call as soon as the previous call is concluded. These are good features if the TSRs are only answering questions. But they can create a problem if the TSRs have paperwork to complete after each call.

- **Power Backup:** What accommodations for power failure does the system offer? Will all the data in the system's memory be lost after a power outage of a second, 30 seconds, an hour, etc.? What happens to the operating system? Can calling continue without power?

- **Internal Functions:** Can calls be transferred from one operator to another? Can a third party, such as the supervisor, join the conversation? Can one call be put on hold while another call is taken? Can TSRs make direct outside calls, or must they go through an operator?

- **Call ID:** Can the TSR identify an incoming call through a visual display or audio signal? Such a capability can be very useful if the telemarketing center serves several marketing objectives, such as sales, service, research, and so on.

When shopping for an ACD, you may come across the terms Uniform Call Distributors (UCD) and Automatic Call Sequencers (ACS). UCDs distribute calls to TSRs by a programmed priority system. These systems are not as flexible as ACDs. The ACS systems usually answer all calls with a programmed message and then flash a signal to the TSRs.

So far we've only discussed hardware and software which routes calls in and out of your place of business. Technology has moved light years further. There is now a wide array of equipment that can answer questions or direct calls to the correct party. Most of these devices are primarily suited for inbound telemarketing centers, but outbound callers can utilize them to manage callbacks.

The most common of this group of products is the automatic receptionist or interactive voice response system. We've all run into one . . . "If you'd like to place an order, touch 1 now. If you'd like to speak to someone in service, touch 2 now." Or you may get a message asking if you have the proper information available before you are connected to a TSR.

The next generation of this type of equipment actually answers callers' questions. These are very commonly used by large financial institutions—banks, in particular. What they do is give the calling party access to all or part of a database. You can call your bank to check the balance of your credit card or checking account, for example.

Some of these will additionally allow the caller to request information to be sent, or even a fax. For example, at an investment firm I worked with, the accounts could call to request our daily outlook on the futures markets. If they liked what they heard, they could ask for a copy of our trading recommendations to be faxed to them. Or they could ask for the fill prices on orders they had placed during the day. This equipment gives them 24-hour access to their account information.

A word of caution: sophisticated precautions must be taken to protect your database from unauthorized access. Keep the storage media, which outsiders access, separate from the storage media on which your private company business resides. By separate, I mean a different computer, or on a network that cannot be accessed through a modem. It is important that inbound callers cannot get access to one of your outbound lines. Hundreds of thousands of dollars of long-distance calls are fraudulently charged to companies this way each year.

Also, you have to assume that at some point the information outsiders can access will become public. For example, an investigative reporter obtained the Social Security number of a public official from the tax return he made public. With this number, he accessed this official's stock dividend account and published the details.

When you set one of these systems up, brainstorm how it might backfire on you. Some financial firms include a "release from damages" as part of their account forms to protect themselves. Their clients also have a choice of whether their information can be accessed this way or not. Not only the famous have had problems, as some people going through a contested divorce have learned.

You might be thinking that this technology is too expensive, except for only the largest companies. But prices are dropping radically. Also, I have seen two or three noncompetitive companies in adjacent offices joint-venture a system. Don't overlook the possibility of setting up an inexpensive computer bulletin board or voice mailbox system for your customers. These are great ways to exchange orders, shipping schedules, pricing, specs, and a whole lot more. The objective is to find ways to best utilize your TSRs, so they are doing things only people can do.

When selecting your equipment, try to match, as closely as possible, the features offered by the system to the needs of your center. Take the time to identify all your requirements, current as well as future, before starting your search. Since these systems generally range in price from $20,000 to more than $500,000, depending on size and configuration, choosing the one best suited to your telemarketing center is of the utmost importance.

ON-THE-LINE MONITORING

As mentioned earlier, the monitoring of TSR calls by a manager or supervisor can be accomplished through the standard conference call feature found on many phone systems. On some key-set phones, the manager can listen in on a TSR simply by pressing the key of the line the TSR is using. In most small centers (five or fewer TSRs), just sitting next to the TSR when he or she is making calls may be sufficient.

Managers of larger telemarketing centers should consider installing a more elaborate monitoring system, because the ratio of callers to managers is higher and the levels of experience of the TSRs vary more. Usually a monitoring function is an integral feature of call distribution systems. At present, some state and federal regulations restrict this practice because of how closely it resembles wiretapping. It invades the privacy of the call, especially if the party being called is unaware of the third party listening.

Some telemarketing managers tape record sales calls and critique them at a later time with TSRs. The use of a tape recorder, however, requires that the person being called be alerted to the fact that the conversation is being taped. This is accomplished with a beeper signal every 15 seconds. The constant interruption of this sound can make the taped calls virtually useless for training purposes. An attorney familiar with these issues and your state laws should be consulted before a monitoring or taping.

Some points to consider when deciding whether or not to install a monitoring system:

1. Is it silent? Will any noise be detected by either the caller or the person receiving the call? A more normal, relaxed performance by the TSR will result if he or she is unaware of being observed. Furthermore, the prospect may quickly terminate the call if he or she believes the call is being monitored by a third party or being recorded. This is a serious flaw in monitoring calls on a key-type phone system—the sounds of lines switching and background noises can be easily detected.

2. Will the device work on the existing phone system?

3. Can all the lines in the center be observed from a central location, such as the telemarketing manager's office?

4. Can both sides of the conversation be put on a speaker phone? Listening to experienced TSRs make calls, and discussing them as they are in progress, is an excellent training tool for new TSRs.

5. Can the system expand to accommodate additional TSRs?

6. Is it a good buy? Is it quality equipment with a good warranty from an established company?

Automating Your Telemarketing Center

Your hardware and software choices are plentiful. I'd go as far as to characterize them as overwhelming. For example, should you buy a computer built around the 8086, 286, 384, 486, or 586 computer chip? Should it run at 25, 33, or 66 MHz? Is a math coprocessor needed? Or a 300- or 2400-baud modem? What about networking? CD ROM? 3¹/₂-inch or 5¹/₄-inch disks? Tape or diskette backup? Macintosh- or IBM-compatible? What type of printer suits your operation? Laser, ink jet, dot matrix? All this, and we haven't even discussed which of the hundred or so brands would be suitable.

If you're a little confused by the hardware selection process, you'll be totally snowed when you get to software. *Business Marketing* magazine publishes a reference guide on sales management software, and *Telemarketing* magazine does one on telemarketing software. The difference between these two classes of software is that telemarketing software is usually written for the large (50 or more TSRs) center, while sales management leans toward the smaller operation. If you're a big hitter in telemarketing and are setting up a major service bureau, I'm assuming you are not reading this book to make hardware and software decisions. This text is prepared for the person who is organizing a small telemarketing center, let's say from 1 to 20 TSRs.

Besides the two basic classes of software just mentioned, there are several programs that bridge the gap between sales management and telemarketing. They combine database marketing with telemarketing and follow-up capabilities. Database marketing simply means gathering the information needed by your salespeople to build long-term sales relationships with your customers. Good TSRs are always asking questions, learning more and more each day about individual customer's buying habits, then going back to those clients with the products and services they need. They uncover needs and then match the benefits of their products with them. The database is where the needs of clients and prospects are stored. The information stored can be personal or professional.

The telemarketing part of the software links your TSRs to their customers. It stores phone numbers, dials them, redials them if the line is busy, creates calling lists, and automatically moves your TSRs through the lists.

Follow-up means the ability to generate letters, invoices, fax transmissions, mail lists, electronic mail, etc. Experience has demonstrated that sending something to prospects immediately after sales calls increases response. The same goes for customers, but it doesn't have to be after each call. Therefore, you want your software program with the following:

Telemarketing Features

1. Auto dialing.

2. Calendar/tickler/follow-up call queue for specific periods of time, like a day or a week, but definable by parameters.

3. Scripting or prompts.

4. Call scheduling by market segment, project, or chronologically.

5. Automatic scheduling of callbacks.

6. Assignment of customers to individual TSRs.

7. Alarm to alert TSRs to special callback times.

8. Call activity tracking—i.e., dialings per hour/shift, results, etc.

9. Automatic updates of files following a call or other sales activity.

10. Automatic queue up of next call and customer record.

11. Customer record includes database information, previous sales history, previous call history, and future planned activity. A method to sort sales history, call history, and/or future activity needs to be devised.

12. Speed—system needs to be reasonably fast.

13. Ability to create multiple databases, such as one for customers and another for prospects or new lists you're testing, so you can keep them separate to prevent a database from becoming too unwieldy.

Sales Features

1. Has closed-loop system to prevent losing prospects.

2. Has ability to link related people, prospects, or businesses.

3. Tracks sales history, sales contracts, bids, proposals, etc.

4. Generates reports of sales, appointments, demonstrations, etc., by salesperson, sales team, territory, etc.

5. Has order entry or order-taking capability plus generation of invoices, packing slips, etc.

6. Has ability to browse forward and backward through database of customers or prospects.

7. Has ability to generate reports that evaluate advertising—direct mail, radio, TV, etc.—from source code.

8. Allows users to modify screens to more closely reflect their business.

Software Features

1. Easy data input.

2. Duplicate recognition and elimination at input.

3. Word processing capabilities, particularly the storage and generation of a library of standard letters and reports utilizing database information, plus the ability to insert specific information manually.

4. Ability to easily adjust size of files whenever necessary.

5. Built-in tutorial.

6. Easy to load, operate, and back up.

7. Compatibility with all types and makes of printers.

8. Import/export function for lists and databases.

9. Software functions that handle e-mail, fax, etc.

10. Pop-up calculator.

11. Multiple-year calendar.

12. Ability to move around program with the use of function keys that can be customized.

13. Reminder note pad independent of any record or file.

14. Set-up to print single labels, envelopes, or lists on one-up, two-up, or four-up formats.

15. Ability to print all the first pages of a multiple page letter separately on letterhead from the rest of the letter, which would be on plain paper.

16. Help screens throughout.

17. Default capability for date, city, ZIP, etc., that may be the same for a number of entries made at one time.

18. Word processor that merges with database.

19. Detailed, user-friendly documentation.

20. Automatic data saver that can be turned on and off.

21. Open architecture to allow software to interface with other software packages, like accounting, inventory, etc.

22. Automatic updating of dates and records throughout system.

23. Networkable for up to 20 TSRs.

24. Ability to sort on all fields of the database and produce reports and special lists.

25. A strong and flexible report generator.

26. User-defined database fields.

Telecommunications Features

1. Auto-dialers need basic phone capabilities—hold, three-way conferencing, flash hook, transfer, etc.

2. Electronic mail functions.

3. Facsimile transmission capabilities.

If you think my software shopping list is an impossible dream, think again. Several PC programs commercially available for under $1,000 have all of the above. For example, the one I've used for the last five years is TELEMAGIC by Remote Control, International. It integrates 10 powerful functions: database management, communications, word processing, scheduling, calendar, calculator, order entry, reporting, e-mail, and, most important for telemarketing, online information,

As far as hardware is concerned, I recommend buying as advanced a machine as you can comfortably afford. But you can get by fairly inexpensively, if you must. I helped a client set up a two-person center with refurbished computers at a cost of less than $1,000 per computer and $800 for software. Not bad—and he has all the capabilities described above. We even linked the two computers together so the TSRs can cover for each other and share a single printer.

For printers, your choice depends on how high-quality of a look you need to give your customers and prospects and the amount of graphics you'll be sending them. Laser printers provide the high-

Exhibit 6–2
Telemarketing Software Checklist
Rate the importance of each feature as it applies to your telemarketing center. Use this scale:

> 9 = very important
> 5 = somewhat important
> 1 = not important at all

1. Sorts of phone numbers by time zone
2. Can set call priorities and prepare calendar of activities
3. Updates files
4. Dials numbers and has automatic callback procedure
5. Records call results
6. Provides online access to Reference Guide material
7. Allows online access to customer file and database
8. Tracks call activity
9. Generates statistical reports
10. Checks credit cards for accuracy (correct number of digits) and fraud
11. Handles fulfillment (shipping labels, letters, packing slips, invoicing, inventory adjustments, etc.)
12. Maintains and generates mailing lists in various formats (cheshire or pressure-sensitive labels, 3"× 5" cards, data bank audit reports, etc.)
13. Prepares performance reports as desired on each TSR and combines results of entire staff
14. Is user-friendly, menu-driven with help screens
15. Is flexible enough to make simple modifications to the program (customization of database screens, script changes) without additional programming
16. Is compatible with various list formats, such as magnetic tape and floppy disks
17. Has the capability to expand the number of stations online, increase memory, and add unlimited number of projects
18. Offers a quick and easy backup system
19. Has password control and other security protection

Exhibit 6–2 (continued)

20. Provides locater function by contact's last name, first name, ZIP code, area code, and phone number
21. Has the capability to eliminate duplicate files
22. Can profile customers by demographics
23. Is able to handle inbound and outbound calls simultaneously
24. Each terminal performs different functions simultaneously (date search, print, etc.)
25. Has proven track record in similar sized telemarketing centers
26. Can load tape for merge/purge operations with other lists
27. Can download external files (census track information, for example) to enrich in-house data bases and customer files

---

est-quality look, especially when there are a lot of drawings, charts, graphs, etc. If all you send is simple follow-up or thank you letters, you can get by with a dot matrix printer, but make it at least a 24-pin printer. If you need color in your graphs to stand out from the crowd, consider an ink-jet printer.

Don't forget: when budgeting for equipment, you'll need phones, headsets, and modems to get online. And probably a copy machine as well.

If you have more than one TSR, should you network their computers together? The advantage is they share the database. For example, if TSR "A" is online with a customer and another call comes in for her, TSR "B" can take the call. If they share information, "B" handles the call. If not, it may result in a callback at best and a lost order at worst.

Ideally, when a call is received, the TSR can make a few keystrokes while making some small talk and instantly have the client's record on screen. A quick scan of the data allows the TSR to intelligently handle the call.

Another big advantage of networking is the ability to share expensive peripheral equipment, such as a $1,500 laser printer.

But you can also get by with less expensive switch boxes, around $100, that allow your people to share devices.

The concern with networking is that it requires a slightly higher level of computer expertise than using independent machines. Also, if the network goes down, all your staff is down. On the other hand, if you are comfortable with computers or have a skilled technician on staff, there are many advantages. TELEMAGIC has a network version, as most good software programs do, but it costs about twice as much. Therefore, you must budget for higher costs if you plan to network.

Consumer Telemarketing Automation

If you plan to do telemarketing primarily to consumers, you should look at equipment that includes predictive dialing. Carefully designed algorithms drive computers to dial slightly more numbers than there are telemarketers. These mathematical formulas calculate the number of call attempts that will be answered and switches calls to the TSRs the instant they are answered. Busy and unanswered dialings are recycled for another attempt at a later time.

The result is that your staff receives a steady flow of prospects. They are spared the frustration of dialing 5, 10, 20 or more times to talk with one person, which can often happen with consumer calling. This can be a particular problem with daytime canvassing, since there is such a large percentage of families today in which everyone works. With predictive dialing, you can economically do daytime calling for some products and services. Additionally, you need substantially fewer TSRs to go through the same size list. And the TSRs do a better job of presenting your story, because predictive dialing allows them to develop a rhythm.

Predictive dialing systems are ideal for companies that repeatedly market to certain geographic areas. Cable companies, lawn care, newspapers, fund raising, waste management, photography, etc.—all of these types of services come to mind.

I've always wondered why entrepreneurs haven't set up localized telemarketing service bureaus that specialize in providing telemarketing for organizations that canvass a territory once or twice a year. It would be easy to develop a reference guide for each service and train professional TSRs to promote a wide variety of products and services. This approach could justify the cost of the equipment.

And, once you get a clean list of all the households in a community, you might as well use it as often as possible.

For example, the predictive dialing system is initially loaded with all the numbers in a given area. The first step is to delete all the hospitals, schools, and other emergency numbers. Then you must separate the business numbers from the households. Next, you delete any residence that you know does not wish to get telemarketing calls. Some states have an asterisk law (telephone customers pay to have an asterisk printed in front of their name in the phone directory, for example). Don't forget those that ask to be dropped from your list, as per the Telephone Consumer Protection Act.

Another common feature of these systems is that they perform most of the clerical work and call accounting. One vendor I'm familiar with has an excellent product and has been at this business for over a decade. It's TeleDirect International, Inc. They produce a well-thought-out and dependable system.

Summary

There are so many advantages—i.e., better service, lower costs, smarter marketing—to automating your telemarketing center that there is no reason not to consider it from the start. You even have the advantage of doing it at a time when hardware prices are still declining. It simply costs less to be more productive now than any other time in the history of telemarketing.

Budgeting for the Telemarketing Center

7

There are four primary areas to review when preparing a budget for a telemarketing center: the sales forecast, expenditures on capital assets, fixed costs, and variable costs.

The sales forecast is an estimate of the number of sales, in units and dollars, expected to be made over the period covered by the budget.

Capital expenditures include outlays for depreciable assets, such as the acquisition of a building or the renovation/redecorating of existing space, furniture and fixtures, telephone equipment, computer hardware and software, and so on.

Fixed costs are those expenses that are incurred on a regular basis and are not directly affected by the number of calls made or orders taken. They include expenses such as TSR salaries (but not incentive bonuses), rent, equipment leases, monthly telephone service charges (but not long-distance charges), telephone line installation fees, employee benefits, payroll taxes, utilities, office supplies, and management support.

Variable costs are those expenses that are directly related to a center's activity level or sales volume. They include long-distance call charges, TSR incentives and bonuses, overtime pay, fulfillment costs, and product costs.

Budgeting a Model Telemarketing Center

The best way to understand a telemarketing budget is to develop one, which we will do in this chapter.

CREATING THE SALES FORECAST

The first steps in developing a telemarketing budget are determining the size of the prospective market for the product and a forecast of sales based on reasonable assumptions. The size of the potential market is determined by totaling the number of names on all the lists available for that market. Sales estimates are based on the number of calls made to the available names that you might reasonably expect will be converted into orders.

The use of this two-pronged approach—determining both the list universe and the order conversion rate—yields a reasonable sales projection from which fixed and variable expenses can be estimated.

To illustrate, let us assume that we employ one telemarketing manager and four TSRs to sell a $150 product requiring little or no postsales service or support. Assume further that we rent our lists from reliable list brokers who have access to an almost limitless supply of names. (These budget assumptions are based on an actual case history.) Our dialings for the year can be calculated as follows:

4 TSRs × 6 calling hours/day = 24 total calling hours/day

24 calling hours/day × 5 days/week = 120 total calling hours/week

120 calling hours/week × 50 weeks/year = 6,000 total calling hours/year

6,000 calling hours/year × 15 dialings/hour (our assumption for a manual center) = 90,000 dialings/year

6,000 total calling hours/year × 30 dialings/hour (in an automated center) = 180,000 dialings/year

Since these are dialings and not completed sales presentations or orders, we now must assume further that it will take a TSR four dialings to make one completed call—a relatively conservative estimate for a business-to-business product. A manual telemarketing center would make 22,500 sales presentations a year (90,000 dialings divided by 4) and an automated center 45,000 (180,000 divided by 4).

If we also assume that the TSRs experience a closing rate of 20 percent, which is not uncommon for a well-targeted product in the $150 price range, then estimated annual unit sales from this effort would be 4,500 for the manual center (20 percent of 22,500 presentations) and 9,000 for the automated center (20 percent of 45,000). The gross sales figures for the manual and automated centers would then be $675,000 (4,500 × $150) and $1,350,000 (9,000 x $150), respectively. Since we also must assume that 15 percent of the customers may return the product or not pay for it, net sales for the year would be $573,750 for the manual center and $1,147,500 for the automated center. (The results of the sales and cost calculations for a manual center are shown on the summary budget.)

VARIABLE EXPENSES

A telemarketing center's largest variable costs generally are its long-distance charges, the cost of goods sold, and fulfillment. Since the cost of goods sold and fulfillment costs for a telemarketing center are no different than for any other kind of business operation, we will focus most of our attention on long-distance charges. For the purpose of our model budget, cost of goods sold is $34.50 per unit (23 percent of the sales price) and fulfillment is $3 per unit.

As we have established in our sales forecast, the four TSRs are presumed to make calls for a total of 500 hours a month and 6,000 hours a year. We also assume that approximately half the time TSRs spend calling is actual online time billable by the telephone company. This translates into 250 billable hours a month and 3,000 for the entire year.

	Monthly	**Annually**
Long-Distance Service	$3,000	$36,000

Long-distance charges vary widely, as the following table illustrates, because of the breakup of AT&T. These are actual price quotations I received from two primary carriers and two resellers, which broker long-distance for the major carriers. Basically, resellers are marketing firms that contract for large amounts of long-distance time at very low prices and resell it. Supposedly, the only drawback to buying from a reseller is that if a problem occurs, they are in line for assistance behind primary customers. But I am unaware of any instance of a secondary user being without service for a long period of time. For our budget, I used a conservative figure of 20 cents per minute.

Survey of Long-Distance Rates
(Cents per Minute)

Miles	Day/Evening	Day/Evening	Day/Evening	Day/Evening
0-292	14.4/10.8	17.9/16.3	19.6/13.9	22.3/18
293-430	16.2/12	19.3/16.3	20.0/14.8	23.0/19
431-925	17.4/13.2	20.1/16.3	22.0/16	23.5/19.3
926-1,910	18.6/13.8	21.2/16.3	23.0/16.8	24.3/20
1,911-3,000	19.2/14.4	21.2/16.3	23.0/17.5	25.0/20.3

Another variable cost is the sales incentive for TSRs. Based on certain industry standards, $2 per calling hour, or $12,000 a year in our example, would be a realistic budget estimate. Whether the entire incentive allocation is distributed depends on TSR performance.

FIXED EXPENSES

The fixed costs include salaries/wages and associated employee benefits for the telemarketing manager and the TSRs, monthly line charges, office rent and utilities, supplies, support materials such as telemarketing reference guides, and so on.

Staff Costs—In our example, salaries, wages, and employee benefits would be budgeted as follows:

	Monthly	Annually
Telemarketing manager/supervisor	$2,500	$30,000
4 TSRs ($6/hr. × 40 hrs./wk. × 52 wks./yr. × 4 TSRs)	$4,160	$49,920
Fringe benefits (25% of wages)	$1,665	$19,980
Total	$8,325	$99,900

A $30,000 yearly salary for the manager of our relatively small telemarketing center is unusually high, adding $5 an hour in cost for each of the 6,000 hours of calling a year. In most real business situations, the telemarketing manager is given additional responsibilities, such as assistant sales or marketing manager, to help defray some of the cost of his or her salary. In such cases, only a portion of the telemarketing manager's $30,000 salary is charged to the telemarketing center. A capable and experienced telemarketing manager can directly supervise up to 50 TSRs and possibly more if he or she has some good team leaders among them.

The $6 per hour rate for TSRs is average for the central United States but could vary substantially depending on local wage levels and the type of product being sold. Likewise, fringe benefits could vary considerably from the 25 percent of salary estimate in our example.

Space Costs—In our example, monthly rent for office space is budgeted at $1 per square foot per month. Maintenance, utilities and other related overhead are an additional $.50 per square foot per month.

	Monthly	Annually
TSRs (100 sq. ft. × 4 TSRs × $1.50)	$600	$ 7,200
Telemarketing manager's office (225 sq. ft. × $1.50)	$337.50	$ 4,050
Total	$937.50	$11,250

List Costs—Of course, for any telemarketing center to begin operations, a list of prospects must be acquired. Keeping four TSRs actively calling six hours a day for the year requires an estimated 50,000 names, allowing for at least two attempts (dialings) on each name. The names would be ordered in batches of approximately 4,000–5,000 per month, according to sectional center postal codes (the first three numbers of the ZIP code) or telephone area codes, to provide for a balance of names in each time zone. Ordering lists this way also helps eliminate the problem of renting duplicate names from the same list source. We assume that list rental costs would be $125 per thousand names.

	Monthly	**Annually**
Names @ $125/M		
(4,167 names/mo., 50,000/yr.)	$520.83	$6,250

Telemarketing Reference Guide—For budgeting purposes, the cost of developing the center's telemarketing reference guide also is considered a fixed expense, since its cost is not directly related to the center's calling or sales volume. Preparing such a guide can take anywhere from 4 to 40 hours depending on the detail desired and the accessibility and quality of the material available to develop it. Most centers prefer to develop their own reference guides, but they can be professionally written by an ad agency or independent telemarketing consulting specialist at a cost of $1,000 to $2,500. In our example, however, we assume that the telemarketing manager spends an entire work week preparing the center's telemarketing reference guide. Its cost, therefore, is already included in the telemarketing manager's salary and fringe benefit figures.

CAPITAL EXPENDITURES

The establishment of any new telemarketing center requires several significant up-front capital expenditures on office furnishings and telecommunications equipment. The following budget is a fair representation of what these expenditures might be for the center in our example.

Remodeling of existing space	$1,000
4 TSR desks with chairs plus the telemarketing manager's desk and chair	2,500
2 filing cabinets	500
4 TeleEasels	250
4 headsets	500
5 phones	1,000
4 portable partitions to separate TSRs	400
Total:	$6,150

The telephone system we are planning for our model center will operate up to six lines and have a conference call feature to allow the telemarketing manager to monitor TSR calls. If the center expands at a later date, a dedicated monitoring system can be added.

One important question is whether to automate the center at its inception. We decide to begin with a manual system, since there will be enough to learn and manage initially without the added burden of trying to computerize the center.

If all works as planned and our first telemarketing efforts are successful, we may be able to computerize the operation and thereby effectively double its efficiency without adding personnel. We estimate the cost of doing so to be between $25,000 and $50,000.

The center's capital expenditures—$6,150—are represented in the budget by the depreciation expense: $105 per month, or $1,230 annually.

SUMMARY BUDGET PRESENTATION

Based on the assumptions and calculations presented above, here is the monthly and annual budget for our model telemarketing center.

Model Telemarketing Center Budget for a Manual Center

	Monthly	Annually
Gross Revenues	$56,250	$675
Less Returns and Bad Debt (15%)	(8,438)	(101,250)
Net Revenues	$47,812	$573,750
Fixed Expenses:		
Salaries and Benefits	$8,325	$99,900
3 Local Phone Lines	110	1,318
Rent and Utilities	938	11,256
List Rental	521	6,250
Capital Assets		
(depreciated over 5 years)	105	1,260
Total Fixed Expenses	$9,999	$119,984
Variable Expenses		
Long-Distance Charges	$3,000	$36,000
TSR Incentives	1,000	12,000
Cost of Goods		
($34.50/unit)	12,940	155,250
Fulfillment ($3/unit)	1,125	13,500
Federal Telephone Tax	*105	1,290
Miscellaneous	1,000	12,000
Total Variable Expenses	$19,170	$230,040
Contribution to Company		
Overhead and Profit	$18,643	$223,726
Percent of Gross Margin	33%	33%

* You may also have to budget local and state taxes on the phone service in your area.

The center's break-even sales figure for the year would be 1,571 units, calculated as follows:

Net Sales:	$573,750
Variable Costs:	(230,040)
Gross Margin:	$343,710

Gross Margin of $342,710 divided by Unit Sales of 4,500 = $76.38 Gross Margin Per Unit

Fixed Costs of $119,950 divided by Gross Margin Per Unit of $76.38 = 1,571 Units Break-Even

This means that based on the projected 6,000 calling hours for the year, the center must make 0.26 sales every hour (1,571 units divided by 6,000 calling hours) or one sale every four hours or so to break even. In dollars, the center's break-even per calling hour would be approximately $40 (1,571 × $150 price per unit divided by 6,000 hours).

Use the checklist at the end of this chapter as a guide to planning and budgeting a telemarketing center.

Testing Telemarketing Assumptions

After a budget has been developed, uncertainties about some of the assumptions are bound to arise. Can 15 dialings per hour be accomplished and maintained? Will every fourth call result in a completed call? Is a 20 percent close rate reasonable? What if returns exceed the 15 percent budgeted? Are three long-distance lines too many or too few? Would adding an inbound toll-free number be cost-effective? And so on. (See Exhibit 7–1.)

One way to answer these questions before you take the expensive and risky plunge into starting the center is to develop a test project with a professional telemarketing service bureau. Develop a test campaign that resembles as closely as possible the conditions that would exist if you decided to bring the campaign in-house. Use the same lists and the same number of TSRs. You can develop the reference guide yourself or have the agency develop it

Exhibit 7–1
Telemarketing Center Budget Checklist

Office Space Renovation

Furnishings:
_____ Desks
_____ Work stations
_____ Chairs
_____ Filing cabinets
_____ TeleEasels
_____ Partitions
_____ Noise reduction devices (walls, ceilings, floors)

Telephone Equipment:
_____ Headsets
_____ Telephones
_____ Call distribution system
_____ Monitoring system
_____ Telecommunication devices (modems for voice/data transmission)

Automation/Computer System Equipment:
_____ Software
_____ Hardware (CRTs, disk drives, CPUs, printers, etc.)
_____ List conversion equipment

Miscellaneous Office Equipment:
_____ Typewriters
_____ Fax machine
_____ Copiers
_____ Calculators

Fixed Costs Checklist:
_____ Salaries
_____ Wages
_____ Rent

Exhibit 7–1 (continued)

_____ Utilities
_____ Overhead
_____ Equipment leases
_____ Telephone access charges
_____ Federal, state, local, FCC taxes
_____ Telephone line installation
_____ Fringe benefits
_____ Unemployment taxes
_____ Social security taxes
_____ List rental/purchase/compilation
_____ Office supplies
_____ Management support
_____ Reference guide preparation

Variable Costs:

_____ Long-distance line charges
_____ TSR sales incentives
_____ TSR/TM manager bonuses
_____ Overtime wages
_____ Cost of goods sold
_____ Fulfillment
_____ Federal/state/local phone taxes
_____ Credit card charges

---

for you. During the test, plan to spend as much time as possible personally monitoring calls to learn as much as you can about what your staff will face when the campaign is brought in-house.

This kind of test costs between $3,500 and $6,000 if you develop your own reference guide. Most agencies will want to run at least a 100-hour test, at about $35 per hour plus $1,000 to $1,500. for the initial set-up and TSR training. This investment could be well worth the time and expense, since it will allow you to confirm budgeting assumptions, establish and perfect the reference guide, test lists, validate sales scripts, experiment with offers, etc.

FINDING A TELEMARKETING SERVICE BUREAU

How do you shop for a telemarketing agency? What kinds of things should you look for?

Conventional wisdom dictates finding a large agency with years of experience. Keep in mind, however, that experience can be misleading. Five years of varied telemarketing experience certainly can recommend a professional agency. On the other hand, if it has spent five years telemarketing the same product for a single client to the same customers, that equates to one year's experience repeated five times.

Size can be misleading. Bigger is not always better when it comes to telemarketing agencies. Look for a service bureau that listens to you—one that can demonstrate how it has handled marketing problems similar to yours and can explain precisely how it intends to address yours. Try to determine if staff people are genuinely interested in being telephone marketers or are satisfied with simply being purveyors of excess telephone capacity. Look for breakthrough ideas and approaches that might show an understanding of your marketing problems, with the potential to materially improve your business. Question them thoroughly. Find out how well they know their business.

And, even more important, listen to the questions they ask you. Are the questions meaningful? Do they get to the crux of your marketing concept? Look for depth in management and staff. Visit their offices, if possible. Talk with their creative staff and telemarketing production supervisors. You are a professional in your field; they should be professionals in theirs.

Ask to monitor some calls. Do their TSRs have the talent, energy, and capacity to handle your project? This is how you learn firsthand about the quality of TSRs who someday may be representing your company to thousands of prospective customers. Are the telemarketers simply reading scripts verbatim? How do they handle objections? Do they always find and qualify the decision maker? Do they take the first "no" as the final answer? Are they courteous, and do they sound enthusiastic? Do they ask open-ended questions to learn more about the customer and his needs? After an hour or so of monitoring calls, you will learn almost all you need to know in order to make a decision about the agency.

Always ask for written bids when negotiating. Make sure you understand all the charges. For example, some charge a flat start-up fee, which includes TSR training. Others bill for training at half the calling rate. Script and call preparation also may be billed separately.

After the bids are assembled—always compare at least two service bureaus—it is good practice to try to reduce the final price to some common denominator to aid in making the final decision. Cost per calling hour is a good measure, since it really is what you will be paying for. Here is a simplified example:

Agency #1 bids $35 per calling hour and a $500 start-up fee. For 100 hours, that amounts to $40 per calling hour. [(100 hrs. × $35 + $500) divided by 100].

Agency #2 bids $32 an hour for calling, $18 an hour for training, $15 an hour for clerical, and no start-up fee. They bid the job at 100 hours of calling, 10 hours of training, and 10 hours of clerical. This bid comes to $35.30 per calling hour [($32 × 100 hrs) + ($18 × 10 hrs.) + ($15 × 10 hrs.) divided by 100].

If all other extraneous costs are equal, agency #2 is almost 12 percent less expensive. But be certain not to confuse cost with performance. Remember, your number-one objective is usable, measurable, and repeatable results!

8

Integrating Telemarketing into Your Existing Marketing Program

In order to begin integrating telemarketing into your company's existing marketing mix, you first must determine which of the company's products, product lines, or services best suit telemarketing. I suggest you start with a product or service that is relatively uncomplicated and easy to describe, and that requires little or no after-sales support. Preferably it can be bought by a single buyer and does not require a series of decisions at various management levels. A high-priced, complex product or service should be avoided on your first foray into telemarketing.

The rationale for this is clear. An easily described, familiar product significantly reduces TSR training time and creates fewer script problems. Furthermore, selling strategies for such products are easier to develop and implement, and simpler to establish and monitor.

This approach also makes the center's first effort more likely to succeed. An early success is extremely important, since it builds confidence among the center's staff and managers which, in turn, generates increased support for the telemarketing venture. There is nothing like a quick success to convince the most hardheaded "Doubting Thomas" that telemarketing works.

A Multiple-Step Team Approach

For a company that markets only complex products or services, the preceding advice might seem to be of little value. However, there are effective telemarketing strategies for these kinds of products as well. Such methods usually break the telemarketing process down into discrete steps. For example, an initial call identifies decision makers. The next call stimulates interest by offering sales literature and/or special reports. The third and fourth calls obtain a request for proposal, bid, or sample.

It is easy to see how this kind of effort can add to the complexity and cost of operating a telemarketing center. Yet this approach to selling a complex product by phone can often be far more productive than direct mail or even person-to-person sales. It provides direct, interactive contact with the potential customer, which direct mail does not. Furthermore, it can reach a greater number of potential buyers in a shorter period of time and at a significantly lower cost than a field sales force.

Another popular approach to complex selling is the team concept, using TSR trainees as cold-callers or "fronters." The trainee's job is to qualify as many leads as possible, who will then be called by or transferred to more experienced telemarketers.

A typical scenario for the team approach might be for a fronter to elicit what are called "closing questions" from a potentially interested prospect. "Can your product change the strategic direction of my business? Will it improve sales, eliminate paperwork, increase profits, and pay for itself in the first month?" Unable to adequately field these questions, the cold-caller would say, "Allow me to get Mary O'Neil on the phone. She's an expert in this area and will be able to better answer all your questions." At this point, Mary, an experienced telemarketer, picks up the call, answers the prospect's questions, and tries for a close.

Where Should the First Telemarketing Efforts Be Focused?

Although we have been recommending the path of least resistance as the fundamental strategy in the start-up phase of telemarketing, the best accounts should not be the ones to approach first. Begin with marginal accounts—that is, with accounts you can afford to jeopardize should something go wrong on the call. Wait until your system is thoroughly debugged and your people fully trained before telemarketing to your important accounts.

Finding Realistic Telemarketing Opportunities

As you begin to think about integrating telemarketing into your firm's overall marketing program, it is important to remember that telemarketing serves you best when its strengths are applied to appropriate tasks. Throughout this book, telemarketing has been characterized as a direct-contact, mass-market sales tool that can enrich a company's marketing mix by extending its sales reach and providing it with additional low-cost selling opportunities. The following questions are designed to focus your thinking about its potential benefits as they relate to your firm's current marketing environment.

1. Is the frequency of customer contacts important to the product's market penetration?

2. What percentage of accounts produce the bulk of sales?

3. What percentage of selling time are field reps spending on lower-producing accounts?

4. What percentage of field rep time is being spent on taking orders and cold-calling?

5. What is the average cost of a field rep sales call on a marginal account?

6. Does the product or service have potential secondary or tertiary markets that are not being served currently, but would be profitable if sales costs were lower?

7. Are there any new sales territories you should consider? This could include new industries you are not selling to, as well as new geographical areas.

8. Is objective, high-quality, useful research coming in from the field?

9. Is direct mail becoming a less efficient means of selling your products and/or services?

These are the questions that may lead to areas in which telemarketing can profitably contribute to your bottom line. Since telemarketing is a flexible, highly efficient, low-cost source of sales, it can serve you well in those areas in which your current program is inefficient. In some instances, telemarketing may be able to entirely replace your company's more traditional methods of selling—but this is rare. However, there are very few instances in which telemarketing cannot make at least some positive contribution to a company's selling efforts.

How Not to Reinvent the Marketing Wheel

If a certain sales technique has proven successful for your firm over the years, it is likely that the same approach also will work in a telemarketing program. For example, it is obvious that a situation in which the field sales force successfully sells an industrial cleaner by performing onsite demonstrations cannot be exactly duplicated by telemarketing. Yet the telemarketer can call the purchasing agent or decision maker, obtain a commitment to test a free sample, and follow up as often as is appropriate to get an order.

Providing a free sample may seem an expensive proposition. But when the cost of sending a sample drum of a cleaner to the customer is compared with the cost of an onsite demonstration by a sales rep, the benefits of offering the free sample become clearer.

Another approach for selling the cleaner might include a direct-mail promotion or a letter from the firm's sales manager introducing the firm and the telemarketer to the customer. This would be followed by a phone call (see Exhibit 8-1 for a sample letter of introduction). Direct mail and telemarketing are extremely effective together.

The personal letter, by the way, can be a useful adjunct to almost any telemarketing situation. Many companies have their TSRs send follow-up letters to customers after every completed call (see Exhibit 8-2). The objective is to build rapport between the TSR and the buyer. Some companies like to print the TSR's photo on his or her stationery, thus helping make the telemarketing call more personal.

Another interesting telemarketing sales situation involves collecting data from prospective customers that can be used to develop a bid or proposal. Telemarketing service bureaus often use this technique to sell their own telemarketing services. In the initial contact, the TSR asks the prospect to complete a "Five-Minute Market Survey." When completed, it provides the telemarketing firm with a quick overview of the prospect's company, industry, markets, opportunities, products, and problems. The prospective client is asked to return the completed profile along with samples of his or her company's sales literature and other promotional materials.

Exhibit 8–1

TSR Letter of Introduction

Name
Company Name
Address
City, State, ZIP
Date

Re.: Announcing . . . New FREE Consulting Service!

Dear Preferred Customer (personalized, if possible):

We began doing business 22 years ago. One business principle true then is even more pertinent today: there is no substitute for reliable service!

We at [name of the firm] really believe this. That's why we make what we feel are among the finest industrial cleaners available on the market today. Additionally, we . . .

- Offer our products at the lowest prices available
- Use our own trucks to assure delivery within 48 hours of ordering
- Offer a 100% money-back guarantee of satisfaction.

And now, I'm proud to announce an *all new service* . . . TOLL-FREE telephone consulting. Starting today you can simply call us, at no cost to you, at your convenience (during normal business hours, of course), to have any questions about our products answered immediately.

You can, for example, call for an instant cost estimate. Or, to find out how long it will take to get a free delivery. Or, to find the answer to just about any question you may have about using our cleansers in your plant. Here is our TOLL-FREE number:

1-800-123-4567

We have hired two very special customer service people, Jim Robertson and Ann Smith, who have been extensively trained in all aspects of the manufacture and use of our cleaners. Their primary mission is to answer any questions you may have about any cleaning problem.

Jim and Ann will be in touch with you periodically to see if you are having any cleaning problems that we may be able to help you solve. I am sure you will find them helpful and knowledgeable.

Sincerely,

Dick David
Sales Manager

Exhibit 8–2
TRS Sales Follow-Up Letter

Dear ——————————:

I enjoyed our conversation the other day. As you know, my job is to help you as much as I can and make your buying decision for industrial cleaning material as easy as possible. Here are just a few of the things I can offer you:

- Free delivery of your orders—overnight, if necessary (we normally ship within 48 hours of receiving an order);
- Free information and research on solving industrial cleaning problems;
- And the highest-quality cleaning product available, at extremely competitive prices.

I am here to help you save money and make sure your dealings with us are fast, easy, and even enjoyable. So please do not hesitate to call me any time on our TOLL-FREE number: 1-800-123-4567.

Sincerely,

[name]
Cleaning Consultant

P.S. I've taken the liberty of enclosing a few stickers with our TOLL-FREE phone number on them. Please put them someplace on or by the phone, so you'll always have my number handy.

The information and materials are reviewed by the marketing team at the telemarketing firm. The account executive is then prepared to talk intelligently about the client's particular marketing needs in a personal sales call. The prospect receives a "free" marketing consultation with an expert. This approach works for any type of consulting business.

The process of incorporating what already works for your product into your telemarketing effort is simple. Following is a list of the important objectives of any sale. Telemarketing can be used to accomplish any or all of these objectives. Use the list to determine how each of these tasks has traditionally been undertaken by your firm. Then determine which of them can be profitably improved through telemarketing.

1. Find the real decision makers.

2. Develop a personal relationship with your customers.

3. Uncover needs.

4. Match those needs with your product's benefits.

5. Prove the product can satisfy those needs.

6. Obtain orders.

7. Manage after-sales service.

This chapter has attempted to provide some insight into how telemarketing can be used to supplement and enhance your company's marketing efforts. The important lesson to bear in mind when applying telemarketing to your own particular situation is not to abandon what already works, but rather use telemarketing to make it work even better.

9

Telemarketing Follow-Up Systems: The Importance of the Call Report

It is extremely likely that most, if not all, of a company's existing support systems—the systems that form the infrastructure of the day-to-day operations—can accommodate the needs of a telemarketing center. Order processing, warehousing, fulfillment, accounts receivable, customer service, and the like may require only slight changes to respond fully to your new telemarketing capability. Nevertheless, to minimize confusion and to prevent the "tail wagging the dog," it is important to understand how telemarketing can subtly alter existing operating procedures.

A case in point: an investment advisory service had been selling its newsletters through direct mail. Included in its direct-mail package was a money-back guarantee, an order form, and the usual sundry assortment of sales letters, brochures, lift letters, etc. When an order form was returned, the new subscriber was dutifully sent an invoice. The subscriber then paid the amount indicated on the invoice, was entered on the subscription rolls, and began receiving the newsletter.

The investment advisory firm then decided to switch to telemarketing, assuming that this seemingly innocuous change in the mode of delivery of the sales message would not alter its long-established operating procedures. They were wrong!

Within a few weeks of the change, complaints began to pour in. Analysis revealed that although the direct mail and telemarketing messages were very similar, they were being perceived quite differently by customers.

The direct mail piece declared, "Order now and we will enter your subscription!" It also stated that an invoice would be sent, and new subscribers should pay only if they were satisfied. If not, they could write "void" on the bill and return it in the postage-paid envelope.

The telemarketing script, on the other hand, read: "We'd like to send you a copy of our newsletter for your review, can we do that?" Then, later in the conversation, the TSR would say to the prospect, "Along with the review issue, you'll receive some billing information allowing you to accept or decline the special charter rate of $495. A savings of $100!"

In telemarketing, there is a delay between the time the prospect accepts the offer and the time the product arrives with the invoice. Without anything to refer to—no cover letter or acknowledgment—the new subscriber only remembers having agreed to review an issue of the newsletter. "Billing information" is not interpreted by prospects as an "invoice," and, consequently, potential subscribers were not pleased.

All of this could have been avoided had the investment advisory firm immediately sent confirmation letters to new subscribers as a standard follow-up procedure. With direct mail, the new subscriber had before him written material that fully explained the offer. With telemarketing, all he had was a dim recollection of a brief conversation.

The moral of the story is clear: always try to understand the mechanics of any telemarketing sales effort from the customer's point of view. Keep in mind that the only representation of your sales offer to the customer is a disembodied voice at the other end of a telephone line. Problems like those described above usually can be solved easily enough by adding a second or third step to the sales procedures. Such additional procedures usually involve a more detailed follow-up, such as a letter of confirmation that mails the same day the call is made.

The Call Report

A Call Report Form of some sort usually is considered an essential part of any well-managed telemarketing center. Although it adds to a TSR's paperwork, the report should be diligently filled out by every TSR after every call. It can be fully automated, as we learned when discussing sales management software. It illustrates all the basic information associated with each customer or prospect, including notes on every TSR contact with the company. The sample form (see Figure 9–1) can be easily modified to meet your specific needs.

The sales cycle finder on the bottom of the Call Report Form is designed to help a TSR track a customer's sales and optimally schedule calls to the customer. It is especially useful in those situations in which repeat sales occur on a periodic basis. By circling the week of every month in which a sale to the customer is made, a TSR determines the customer's ordering pattern and adjusts the calling schedule accordingly. In most cases, it makes the most sense to call the customer in the week before an order is expected. You want to shut out competition.

Manual call reports usually are filed alphabetically by customer name in three-ring loose-leaf binders or on a TeleEasel. The space for the company name in the upper right-hand corner of the form enables a TSR to quickly flip through the binder to find a report when an inbound call comes in unexpectedly. To make this system work, each TSR's call reports must be accurate and thorough. The telemarketing manager must take the time to review them on a regular basis.

Other Follow-Up Material

The most common form of follow-up material used by telemarketing centers is a series of standard sales letters and/or brochures. TSRs save considerable time by using standard sales letters—all they have to do is fill in the blanks—and thus are able to make more calls (see Exhibit 9–1).

It is not uncommon to have TSRs handle their own clerical work. If the center is computerized, much of it can be performed automatically. Manual systems, however, can be effective. One shortcut that works well is providing the TSRs with half-sized (8½" × 5½") personalized stationery, which they use for handwritten notes to prospects or customers. This saves the time and the cost of typing letters. Most people these days are not offended by a handwritten note, especially when expedited service is the result. Again, you can add a personalized touch by printing the TSR's photograph on the letterhead.

The objective of all these procedures is to find every shortcut you can to encourage TSRs to follow up with customers, but also give them a full six hours every day on the phone. The follow-up system must be well organized, not only to prevent lost calling time but also to ensure that customer follow-up is done in a timely fashion.

Below is a brief checklist for a newly introduced telemarketing program. What adjustments need to be made to the following?

1. Field sales contacts with customers

2. In-house order taking

3. Order processing

FIGURE 9–1

Sample Telemarketing Call Report Form (Front side)

TSR initials   Company Name

Field Account Person (if applicable)   Account #

[   ] Customer   [   ] Prospect   [   ] Other

Mailing Address   Shipping Add., if different
Address: _____   _____
City: _____   _____
State: _____ Zip: _____   _____ Zip: _____
Phone: (_____) _____   (____) _____
Credit Rating: _____   Best time to call: _____ / _____
Contact Person(s) /Title   Comments: _____
_____   _____
_____   _____

SIC code: _____
Purchased last year: $ _____   Potential: $ _____
Frequency: _____
Dates of last 3 purchases: _____
Size of average purchase: _____
Account Rating:
[   ] key   [   ] medium   [   ] marginal

Product(s) currently purchasing: _____

Competitor(s): _____
Terms, conditions & price schedule: _____

Normal reorder & timing: _____

Comments: _____

FIGURE 9–1 (continued)

Sample Telemarketing Call Report Form (Back Side)

Date: _____

Results of Call: _____

Sales Cycle Finder:

JAN		FEB		MAR		APR		MAY		JUN	
1	2	1	2	1	2	1	2	1	2	1	2
3	4	3	4	3	4	3	4	3	4	3	4

JUL		AUG		SEP		OCT		NOV		DEC	
1	2	1	2	1	2	1	2	1	2	1	2
3	4	3	4	3	4	3	4	3	4	3	4

EXHIBIT 9–1
Sample Letter

(Date) _____

Dear _____ :

    Thank you for the time and information you shared with me the other day on the phone. [At this point, add a sentence that personalizes the letter.] _____

_____

    Enclosed is the Five-Minute Marketing Profile we talked about. Its purpose is to obtain enough background about your company and its current marketing activities so we can intelligently discuss *if and how* telemarketing can be integrated into your current marketing plan.

    First and foremost, everything you write in this profile is totally confidential. It will be used *only* to assist in the development of marketing strategies to increase your sales and market share.

    The sooner we understand your products and your markets, the faster we will be able to provide you with marketing ideas that allow you to take advantage of the savings and increased sales possible through telemarketing—the synergistic combination of planned phone calls with your current marketing mix!

    Sincerely,

_____

Account Executive's Name
[Title] _____

P.S. Please send us any other materials—such as sales literature, annual reports, specification sheets, direct mail pieces, etc.—that you think will give us a better understanding of the products and services your company offers.

4. Credit control

5. Accounts receivable

6. Billing

7. Shipping

8. Service/Parts

9. Customer relations

10

The Telemarketing Reference Guide

A telemarketing reference guide contains all the information a TSR needs when calling or preparing to call. It includes the objectives of the telemarketing campaign, list of customer needs, product features and benefits, customer objections followed by proven responses, product descriptions and applications, background on the organization, personnel, and scripts.

There are three important reasons for developing a telemarketing reference guide:

1. In telemarketing, it is very important for all TSRs to be consistent in what they tell customers. This builds credibility.

2. Telemarketing can be stressful; high turnover is not uncommon. A well-written reference guide reduces training time by as much as 50 percent.

3. Telemarketers are expected to have a significant quantity of information from a variety of sources at the tip of their tongue. They'll occasionally need something to fall back on. Good reference guides put all the facts at their immediate disposal.

The best way to describe a telemarketing reference guide is by example. We'll use one for a small company called Mosby Manufacturing, Inc. Appendix 2 contains a generic telemarketing reference guide you can use as a model when you develop your own.

Overview of the Organization

Section One of our sample telemarketing reference guide contains basic information about Mosby. This would include its history, with special emphasis on the things that make the company unique. Here is an excerpt:

Overview of Mosby Manufacturing, Inc.

Mosby Manufacturing was founded in 1975 by Ken Mosby, president and chief executive officer. Mosby builds electrical and sheet metal subassemblies for a wide range of manufacturers. Most of the parts are purchased (electric wire, bulbs, reflectors, capacitors, etc.) from independent suppliers. Our plant forms housing out of raw sheet metal, fabricates the subassemblies, paints them with primer, and ships them to customers for use on their assembly lines.

Mosby's expertise is in short manufacturing runs. Most of our customers are manufacturers who make a variety of finished products and who usually require subassemblies that are too intricate or troublesome for them to handle in their own plants. Mosby can manufacture these products at or below our customers' costs with 100 percent reliability. We even warehouse small quantities for customers and ship on a just-in-time basis.

This excerpt illustrates the primary elements that should be contained in a typical overview—a brief history of the company and insights into its unique characteristics.

Selling Procedures

Section Two provides the TSRs with an explanation of how the company sells its products or services:

Normal Selling Procedures

Mosby's 12 field salespeople personally meet with nearly 200 owners or general managers of small manufacturers each year. They tour the facilities and introduce and explain Mosby's products and services. Their mission is to determine how Mosby's expertise can be used to satisfy the needs of these customers. The goal of each visit is to convince customers to allow Mosby to bid on their next projects.

In preparing a bid, our production foreman, draftsman, and purchasing agent develop a bill of materials and an estimate of the total production costs. These estimates are given to the salesperson for review. The job is then priced and a formal bid prepared and delivered to the prospect. The salesperson calls on the customer the following week to close the sale.

Although the Overview and Selling Procedures sections of the reference guide are optional, some companies that experience high TSR turnover or employ temporary help find it extremely important. It provides new TSRs with vital background information on the company that will aid them in answering customer queries.

In Section Three of the reference guide, the company's telemarketing objectives should be spelled out. If this requires modifications to the existing selling process described in Section Two, they should be specified here. Also, this section must be updated whenever telemarketing priorities change. The frequency will depend on the company; some firms can maintain the same telemarketing objective for years, while others change weekly.

Telemarketing Objectives

Telemarketing's primary objective is to contact existing customers who buy less than 100 units a year to determine their needs over the next 6 to 12 months. This information will be input into our sales production forecasts. Accounting will provide the list.

Emphasis also will be put on obtaining additional business from these accounts and exploring any upcoming projects Mosby can bid on.

From time to time our priorities for telemarketing may change, but the basic overall objectives specified below remain the same:

A. TSRs will prospect for and qualify new customers, set up appointments, and arrange sales trips for Mosby field sales representatives.

B. Full account management will be provided on small (less than 100 units/year) and medium (less than 500 units/year) accounts. Mosby sales representatives manage the large accounts.

C. Determine new or changing needs of existing and prospective customers.

Customer Needs

Section Four addresses the benefits to the customer of the products and services provided by the company. It should also specify any customer needs not being met.

Filling Customer Needs

Mosby Manufacturing provides a much needed service to its customers by supplying them with reliable components in small quantities for their manufacturing processes at a price far lower than it would cost them to produce the subassemblies themselves. Mosby further serves its customers by inventorying fabricated subassemblies. This relieves our customers of the cost of carrying stock and enables them to purchase on a just-in-time basis. They get high-quality subassemblies at low cost, whenever they need them.

A Typical Example

One of our customers, Easy Pull Trailer, manufactures boat and horse trailers. Mosby builds the trailer taillight assembly and the wiring harness. Easy Pull manufactures over a dozen models of trailers and can build 25 units a week. The taillight assembly is always the same, but the wiring harness varies with each model. The trailers are produced sporadically throughout the year, with a seasonal peak in the spring. Mosby keeps a week's supply of the light assemblies on hand at all times and can add any of the wiring harness variations within a few hours.

The company's agreement with Easy Pull Trailers requires us to deliver a week's supply within 48 hours, which is the time it takes them to build the frames.

This arrangement provides Easy Pull Trailers with an "instant" supply of needed subassemblies to meet unexpected production demands without any prior investment on their behalf in labor or parts.

Questions and Probes

Section Five addresses the kinds of questions and probes the TSRs should use. An important key to selling by phone is guiding the conversation to a successful conclusion. This cannot be done by making declarative statements. Because the presentation is made by phone, the TSR cannot see the reactions of the prospect. TSRs do not know if prospects are paying attention, distracted, or preoccupied. Therefore, they must ask questions to avoid losing the prospect's attention and, thus, control of conversations.

Below are some sample probes intended to uncover a customer's needs and lay the groundwork for a sale. Additionally, your TSRs must always be gathering data to build your database on each customer or prospect.

Open-Ended Questions

"Tell me about your manufacturing process."

"What subassemblies do you use in each stage of your assembly line?"

"What areas of the manufacturing process cause you the most problems?"

"Where do you want to cut costs or reduce inventory?"

Closed-Ended Questions

"How many major steps are in your manufacturing process? What are they?"

"How many_____do you build a day?"

"Would you send me some of your sales literature?"

These are just a few samples of the kinds of questions that should be in the telemarketing reference guide. When we examine scripts later, we will see more clearly how and where these probes fit into the presentation and how and when to use open- versus closed-ended questions.

You may have to prepare different sets of questions for different types of customers—active, inactive, prospective—or for the different industries you serve.

Features and Benefits

Section Six provides the TSR with a list of product benefits. The easiest way to prepare a benefit profile is to list all features and convert each one into an explicit benefit for the customer. Here are some examples:

Mosby Features/Benefits

Feature: Mosby specializes in subassembly work.

Benefit: You can be assured you will be getting the highest quality products and service when you order from Mosby, since this is our only business—to service your subassembly needs the best way we can. We are the experts.

Feature: Mosby carries inventories for its customers.

Benefit: You save precious floor space in your plant, do not have to invest in subassemblies before you need them, and have instant access to the subassemblies whenever you do need them.

Feature: Mosby delivers subassemblies within 48 hours.

Benefit: You never run out of important components, and therefore costly shutdowns are avoided. The money we save you adds to your profits.

Feature: Mosby's prices for short-run subassemblies are less than it would cost you to manufacture them yourself.

Benefit: You save money and, therefore, can price your product more competitively or improve your bottom line.

Objections and Responses

Every sales presentation encounters objections at some point. These must be anticipated by your TSRs. Immediate and appropriate responses give listeners confidence. Pauses cause concern, because listeners think the TSRs are trying to make up answers or are uninformed. Following are some sample objections/responses that appear in the Mosby reference guide.

Objection: You have never seen our subassembly; how could you possibly manufacture it?

Response: You are absolutely correct; we have not seen it. But we can follow blueprints or copy an actual part, both of which we have done hundreds of times. Why don't you send us your specifications? If we don't think we can make the part at least as well as you do now, we'll let you know. If we feel we can do the job, all we'd ask is the opportunity to bid on it—no obligation on your part. Does this sound fair?

Objection: How do we know we can rely on you as a supplier?
Response: That's an excellent question. Please consider doing two things for me. First, I'll give you a list of several of our current customers. Call some of them and ask how reliable we are. Second, if you're still concerned, use us for six months or so, but hold a small inventory of your own subassemblies as a backup. Give us a chance to save you money, but keep an ace in the hole just in case. Can I give you a list of people to call right now?

There are three distinct parts to a response. TSRs first acknowledge that prospects have valid concerns. They must never get embroiled in an argument with a customer or prospect. After acknowledging the objection, TSRs manage the situation by explaining that the problems will be dealt with to the customer's satisfaction.

Finally, once the objections are neutralized, TSRs ask questions to regain control of the conversation and to try to obtain some level of agreement from the customer or prospect. I've also found it very useful to teach TSRs some generic probes to use in response to unexpected or new objections. For example, "Can you tell me how that is important to your operation?" Or, "That's really very interesting. Can you elaborate a little more?" The objective is to keep customers talking so the TSRs can think. Few people can think while they are talking.

The Close

Once TSRs reach some mutual ground with the customer, they should attempt to close the sale, even if it is only a trial close. A trial close is a close that does not work, but does not end the conversation. It is useful to attempt to close often, because this brings out the real objections that must be managed at some point before the sale can be made. Phrases such as "What do you think of that?" or "Is that satisfactory to you?" serve well as trial closes.

Several different types of closes are provided in the follow ing examples and in the Workbook in Appendix 2. Making any of them work relies heavily upon timing, which can be taught. The best time to close is usually when some kind of agreement is elicited from the customer or prospect. This is when TSRs must ask for orders!

Sample Closes

Direct:
Send me the blueprint today and I'll have a bid on your desk in three days. Is that satisfactory to you?

Indirect:
We agree that Mosby may be able to help you. How would you like to proceed from here?

Controlled Choice:
Would you like to ship us the sample component you want us to bid on or should I have one of our trucks pick it up?

The Script

The final part of the reference guide, Section Nine, usually causes the most problems—it contains the actual scripts the TSRs will use.

Generally speaking, there are three types of scripts: (1) verba-tim, or word-for-word; (2) guided scripts that provide words and phrases, but leave room for spontaneous interjections by the TSRs; and (3) outline-only scripts, which put most of the burden of creating the conversations on the TSRs.

WHAT TYPE OF SCRIPT WORKS BEST?

The script approach that works best depends on the product or service being sold, the customers or prospects being called, and, finally, on the experience, training, and skill of the TSRs. The objective is to use the form that permits the TSRs to conduct disciplined conversations. This may mean using one type or blending all three.

My preference is to train TSRs with verbatim scripts while teaching them the key elements of the two other types. With this approach, the TSRs are trained, through role-playing, to become fluent with the verbatim script. They also are given a list of probes to enable them to get conversations back on track if necessary. In addition, signposts are strategically placed throughout the script to enable TSRs to quickly scan through the script, when necessary, so the entire presentation is made.

Elements of all three types are thereby combined: (1) signposts are borrowed from the outline form; (2) the probes are the basic elements of the guided form; and (3) the complete script represents the verbatim form. Here is a sample script.

Mosby Manufacturing, Inc.

Marginal-Customer Script

Approved by_____on____/____/_____

Introduction:

"Good morning/afternoon. This is_____with Mosby Manufacturing. May I speak with _____?" (Company contact)

If no: "When would be a good time to call back?" If you don't have a name or our contact is no longer at the company: "May I speak with the purchasing agent or chief engineer?"

Identify the Decision Maker:

"My name is _____ with Mosby Manufacturing. We've done some contract work for you in the past that has saved you quite a bit of money. Are you the person responsible for contracting for subassemblies with outside suppliers?"

Probes/Fact Finding:

"Do you remember the job we did for you?"
(Describe job if necessary;)
"Do you know about Mosby?"
(If not, explain company.)
"Naturally, we'd like to do some more work for you."
"Do you need any more (refer to previous job)?"
"Are there any short-run subassemblies you feel are costing you too much time or trouble that you'd like to outsource? We'd be happy to provide you a no-obligation bid. Do any come to mind?"

Present Offer/Sales Message:

"Mosby would like to bid on some of your low-run subassembly work. You'd be under no cost or obligation. Simply send us a blueprint or a sample of the part. We will prepare a bid for whatever quantities you desire."

Close:

"What would you like us to bid on?"
(Manage objections. Close again.)

Show Appreciation/Reinforce Decision:

"Thank you for the opportunity to bid on your work. As soon as we get the blueprints, we will prepare a bid for your approval. I'm sure you'll find that we can save you time and money. I'll call you after you've had a chance to review the bid. Thanks again. Have a good day."

EXHIBIT 10–1

Script Checklist

Make sure every script has these elements:

_____ Introduction

_____ Qualifies who the decision maker is

_____ Creates interest

_____ Uncovers customer/prospect needs

_____ Matches needs with product's benefits

Manages the objections of—

_____ • No interest

_____ • No money

_____ • No time

_____ Simple in concept and wording

_____ Written from the customer's or prospect's point of view

_____ Call has a meaningful reason behind it

_____ Variety of trial closes

_____ Thanks customer/prospect for time

Unfortunately, very few sales conversations go as smoothly as scripts. But scripts are a necessity of telemarketing—they serve as training aids for the TSRs and help focus their thinking and conversations before they go online (see Exhibit 10–1).

Reference guides are an extremely important telemarketing tool. Without them, TSRs operate in a vacuum, which ultimately is reflected in their performance and the impression they give of your organization to the public. You only make a first impression once. Take the time and carefully prepare a first-rate reference guide. Hire an outside consultant to help you if necessary; it will be well worth the investment. Remember that the reference guide should not be a static, unchanging document. It needs to be updated regularly—daily, if necessary—with new information and/ or new approaches that have proved successful.

11

Training, Coaching, and Motivating TSRs

The training, coaching, and motivating of TSRs are extremely important and continuous processes. Although we sometimes consider these functions as separate activities, it is often difficult to distinguish one from the other at any given time. Although this chapter focuses primarily on training, it also includes coaching and motivating.

Some Training Considerations

I recommend that any newly hired TSR, even one who has prior experience, should receive at least one week of formal telemarketing training. You should not assume that experienced TSRs know all the basics, nor will they know all the specifics of your telemarketing center or your products.

The first two days of the first week's training focuses on the basics, using the Reference Workbook (Appendix 2) or something similar as the text. The next two days can be used to familiarize TSRs with your reference guide. After day two or three, depending on their experience level and aptitude, you begin to get TSRs on the phone. The fifth and final day should be spent on making and critiquing calls in groups and individually.

In addition, it often helps to put TSRs through the same product education programs used for new field sales or service personnel, especially if the product is technical in nature. You might have them work for a week or two in the parts, sales, or service departments.

The Key to Successful Training

Role-playing is absolutely essential in a TSR training program. The goal is to get TSRs to the point where they know their material instinctively, where they are able to answer just about any question confidently and without hesitation. The more varied the roles— that is, the specific types of sales situations used—the better. This builds confidence.

It is important that the telemarketing manager make the TSRs understand the impact they will have on prospects and customers. The importance of questioning and probing techniques must be emphasized. A good part of the role-playing exercises should be dedicated to this aspect of calling.

THE IMPORTANCE OF PROBING

It's only through probing that TSRs manage conversations. In conventional, face-to-face sales presentations, the salesperson can visually evaluate the prospect's level of interest. In telemarketing, the TSR cannot see the prospect. If a prospect should happen to put a hand over the phone to talk with someone in the office in the middle of the sales presentation, a TSR has no way of knowing.

TSRs have only one sense to rely on—their hearing. That is what makes probing so important. As long as the prospect is talking, TSRs knows they have the prospect's attention. When the prospect is silent, the TSR is out of touch. Probing, therefore, maintains contact with the prospect and keeps the sales presentation on track.

The preparation of effective questions and probes is at the very heart of successful telemarketing. Here are some things both good and bad that you can achieve through probing:

1. **Find facts.** Ask specific questions to obtain specific information:

   "How many tons of sheet metal do you use each month?"

   "What do you consider the shortcomings of last year's audit?"

2. **Control the sales presentation.** Lead the prospect by focusing questions:

   "You said you liked the portable model . . . is that correct?"

   "You feel it best suits your market, right?"

   "How many would you like to receive in your first shipment?"

3. **Flatter the prospect.** Questions can be used to promote a prospect's self-image:

   "How did you accomplish all that in only three months?"

   "Did you design those special features yourself?"

4. **Start an argument.** Sometimes questions irritate prospects, so you need to make TSRs aware of the impact of ill-conceived questions. For example:

   "Why are you for abortion?"

"Do you really think he has a chance of being reelected?"

5. **Bore someone to tears.** If your questions are of no interest to the prospect, you can't expect participation or involvement.

To a busy executive:

"How is the weather where you are?"

To a factory foreman:

"What is your company's marketing strategy?"

6. **Cross-examine.** This can occur during fact finding, especially if TSRs neglect to give the prospect a valid reason for questions and ask them without giving due consideration to the answers. This trap should be avoided. Too many questions too fast is as bad as too few. Such as:

"How many do you make?"

"What color is most popular?"

"Which version sells fastest?"

Questions can evoke negative as well as positive responses in customers and prospects. That is why TSRs must be well trained in this technique. It should be the cornerstone of any role-playing training session.

Behind every question and every statement are certain assumptions, some conscious and some subliminal. Every telemarketing conversation can be perceived three ways: (1) what the TSR means to communicate; (2) what is actually said by the TSR; and (3) what is heard on the other end of the phone.

Each person has individual assumptions and values about life that cannot be overlooked or dismissed. In fact, telemarketers must be especially sensitive to such distinctions, since they cannot immediately detect if a prospect's reaction to a particular question is negative. The puzzled look that appears on a prospect's face when something is said that does not match his assumptions cannot be seen by a telemarketer. The TSR's acute sensitivity to a prospect's responses is all the more important considering the brevity of most telemarketing presentations. There is no time for mistakes, and customers become impatient with TSRs who don't recognize the assumptions underlining their conversations.

It cannot be overemphasized: the key to effective telemarketing is establishing rapport with the prospect. How well do your TSRs communicate in telephone conversations? The only way to know for sure is to stay within earshot of them and actively monitor their conversations.

In addition to training TSRs for routine calls, you must prepare them for various special situations they might face. For instance, competitors might call to find out what your company is doing. Trained TSRs should be able to detect them. Here are some tips:

- Real customers ask general questions. Competitors ask very specific ones that show they know more than they should about the product.

- Make sure the TSRs always immediately ask every caller for his or her name, address, and phone number. You may catch a competitor who is unprepared for this simple, direct question and, not wanting to give a real name, may not respond naturally. If there is any hesitation after this question, the TSR should be cautious of supplying too much information.

- Competitors often pose as a large customer trying to find out what your best prices are or your discounts. The information the "customer" supplies should be checked out before special policies or programs are described.

Establish a strict policy on what information can and cannot be given over the phone. For instance, a good policy to follow on pricing is to give out only list prices, except to known customers. All discounts or other special terms must be put in writing to the prospect. If there is any reason whatsoever to be suspicious, the TSR should not hesitate to make a second call to confirm the initial conversation with the prospect after legitimate interest has been established. You want to make sure the callback number is a real one. Also, you can check with a field salesperson to see if he or she knows the account, look the name up in an industry directory, or check information or a phone book. Make sure your TSRs know who the competition is and what information must be kept private.

One helpful approach is for the telemarketing manager to draw up a list of special situations that TSRs are likely to encounter and prepare reference material. One of the most common and most important of these is finding out on an initial call who the decision maker is. This is often referred to as qualifying the prospect.

Qualifying Prospects

Qualifying prospects is one of the simplest skills to teach and to learn, but oddly enough, many TSRs are reluctant, without proper training, to implement it for fear of hurting the prospect's feelings. The best approach is the most direct one. The TSR simply asks:

"Are you the person in charge of buying steel?"
"Do you buy the software for the data processing department?"
"Are you in charge of the accounting department?"
"Who should I talk to about buying or leasing photocopying machines?"

More often than not, if they are not the decision maker, people are relieved to be let off the hook, and they will gladly transfer the caller to the appropriate person. If they are the decision maker, they are proud of it and will tell your TSRs.

TSRs must learn to ask qualifying questions early and often if they're to avoid spending costly minutes giving the wrong person a sales pitch. They also must be taught to think carefully about the exact words or phrases they use in qualifying decision makers. The more specific the questions, the faster the right person is located. The telemarketing manager must become sensitive to any problems TSRs may be having reaching the decision makers. TSRs are to be as direct and specific as possible.

The following two examples show how an imprecise question (#1) can lead to misinformation, whereas a more specific question (#2) leads to the desired information.

Question #1:
TSR: "Are you the person in charge of maintenance?"
Prospect: "Yeah, I'm the janitor, ain't I?"

Question #2:
TSR: "Are you the person who is responsible for buying janitorial supplies?"
Prospect: "No, I'm the janitor. You should be talking with Ms. Jones in purchasing."

Handling Dissatisfied Customers

Another special situation is dissatisfied customers. It takes advanced skills and training to manage them effectively. In fact, script/reference material should be prepared for this eventuality and made available to TSRs as part of their reference guide.

Dissatisfaction usually is the result of one of three problems:

1. Services or products perceived as being unsatisfactory—did not meet the customer's expectation.

2. Fees considered unreasonable or unjustifiable.

3. Misunderstandings between TSRs or the company and a customer.

Dealing with these problems requires a two-pronged approach. First, acknowledge the complaint, which does not mean agreement; it means letting the customer know you realize he or she is unhappy. Then honestly discuss whether the service, product, or fee was correct in light of the customer's expectations and offer some suggestions for solving the problem. If possible, get the customer involved in working out a solution, as in this accounting office scenario:

Customer: "I'm not paying your bill!"

TSR: "You must have some serious reasons for taking that action. Please share them with me."

Customer: "The monthly accounting reports you prepared for us are always late and incomplete. They're of no value."

TSR: "I understand what you're saying. I'm convinced we can find a solution. Tell me exactly what you need in the report and when. We'll do everything in our power to get you the facts you need when you need them. What do you need first each month?"

TSRs must be in charge when dealing with a complaining customer. They must learn to let the customer vent his or her frustrations while remaining unemotional themselves. They must concentrate on the facts.

Once they've mastered this, it is relatively easy to find a remedy for most complaints. In fact, in some cases these situations can be turned into selling opportunities. But even at their worst, complaining customers must be made to feel that your firm is concerned about the problem and committed to customer satisfaction. And regardless of the outcome of the conversation, the TSR must be trained to thank the customer for calling, no matter how difficult this may be. If your TSRs successfully solve customers' problems, they make friends for life.

Reporting to a Customer

Even seemingly simple duties like returning customers' calls should be well thought out and covered in training. You want your telemarketers to make a professional impression, and nobody practices more than the pros.

It's important for a TSR to report back to a customer, because, if done properly, it can pay big dividends. The TSR becomes a useful resource to customers when he or she reports back to them regularly with valuable information. This is a two-step process:

1. Give the customer the information—what are the facts, what conditions caused the problem, what action will be taken by your company in response, and what the resulting benefits are to the customer.

2. Query the customer to make sure he or she understands and agrees with the answers.

Example: A customer asks a TSR to check her account balance, because a billing statement she received appears incorrect. The TSR checks with accounting and calls the customer back with this answer:

> "Hello, Mrs. Jensen. I'm returning your call regarding the question about your account. I checked with accounting. They said they received your check for $2,500 the day after they closed the books for the month [*why* the problem occurred]. It was posted immediately [the *action* taken in response to the request]. Your balance is now $9,500 [*what* the customer wanted to know]. Does that sound correct?" [getting the customer's *agreement*]
>
> "Great. Is there anything you need now while we're on the phone? By the way, this month we're featuring travelers checks . . . no service charge. Would you be needing any this summer?" [turning a request or complaint into a sale opportunity]

Handling Service Problems

To recap, these three steps constitute a time-tested approach to handling customer service problems:

1. Acknowledge problems. Be sympathetic to their plight. Let them know that you empathize with their frustrations, but they are now in good hands and every measure will be taken to accommodate them.

2. Avoid placing blame. Never denigrate the product, the company, or other parts of the organization.

3. Live up to promises and always keep customers well informed. If you promise to air freight, make sure you ship air freight. If for some reason a promise cannot be kept, notify the customer immediately and explain why. The worst thing a TSR can do is be dishonest with a customer. If a TSR cannot solve a particular problem, he or she must honestly admit that to the customer.

Training for Full Account Management

Full account management is a system in which TSRs are assigned to handle permanent accounts on an ongoing basis. The TSR manages every aspect of the company's relationship with the accounts—service, delivery, invoicing, product problems, and, of course, selling. It's database marketing at its purest.

Although the usual procedure in full account management is for TSRs to call accounts regularly, experience teaches that regular calling becomes more productive when the TSRs can give customers a specific reason for making each call, other than just to ask for another order. Full account management calling must be rehearsed by TSRs and should be an integral part of their training process, especially in the role-playing phase. Creativity on the part of the TSRs can pay off here; they should be encouraged to come up with their own ideas for initiating calls.

A CASE STUDY

A distributor of parts and add-on products for the recreational vehicle (RV) market serves three states, with 200 RV service centers in each state. One TSR is assigned to each state. The company is located in the southern United States. There is year-round business, but spring is the strongest season. At that time, the company employs two part-time TSRs to assist with inbound calls, mostly orders.

In the distributor's reference guide is a special section titled "Making Repeat Customer Calls." The overview of this section states that the purpose of these calls is to make the company an increasingly valuable asset to its customer. The company wants to become the customer's primary source of product and industry information, as well as its principal vendor. The guide motivates the TSR to provide this level of reliable service. The TSR will increase his or her sales by following this practice.

All TSRs spend part of the initial training period in the company's shipping department, where they are thoroughly instructed on product details, such as the differences between a Coleman and an Intertherm RV furnace or the size of the mirror needed when towing a tent camper versus a fifth-wheeler. Furthermore, they regularly participate in training sessions on repair given by the service manager and suppliers.

TSRs are encouraged to acquire campers of their own or to borrow and use the company's. If an employee's camper needs repairs, the company fixes it free of charge, if the employee helps. As this indicates, the company's philosophy—which it wants to instill in its TSRs—is to eat, sleep, and breathe the business it serves.

The company believes that this motivation, along with its genuine desire to be the most informative, most service-oriented RV distributor in the industry, almost guarantees successful sales calls. Each call is made professionally and with a purpose. Customers quickly discover that their time is not being wasted, because they pick up useful information with each call, even if they do not order every time.

The sales manager develops a list of valid reasons for regular calls to customers. The TSRs use this list and develop additional reasons on their own. In weekly meetings, the TSRs share their reasons for calling and their success.

Repeat Sales Calls

Every meaningful sales call has a specific purpose. You must constantly analyze your accounts' buying habits and tailor your calls accordingly. From time to time, you may need a little help "creating" a meaningful reason to call a particular customer. The following checklist may stimulate your creativity.

1. *Introduction of a new product:* Be sure the product will interest the customer. If a service center does not carry, install, or repair air-conditioners, it is silly to call them about a new air-conditioner. Capture this kind of information and record it in your database.

2. *Announcement of a new or improved service:* Determine if the new service will be useful to the customer before calling.

3. *Release of service bulletins:* The bulletin could be one of your own or a vendor's. Of course, be sure to check each customer's sales history and database before the call to make sure the bulletin is relevant.

4. *Price adjustment:* If a price is increasing, contact your customers to give them the opportunity to order at the old price. If it is a price reduction, you'll be the bearer of good tidings.

5. *Inventory sale:* Always help your accounts take advantage of sales specials on items they buy on a regular basis.

6. *Follow-up to information recently sent to a customer:* Keep track on your database of everything you send to your accounts. A follow-up call about your response to a service/delivery problem or a price quotation is an excellent opportunity to show your concern and, possibly, to initiate a new sale.

7. *Analysis of previous purchases:* This often reveals new sales opportunities. For instance, a customer who regularly buys repair parts for heaters might be persuaded to keep at least one portable heater in stock, should they ever require a "loaner" in the case of unavailable parts.

8. *Delivery problems:* If, after taking an order, you learn that one of the products is on back order from the vendor, call the customer back with this information and offer an alternative, if appropriate.

9. *Long lead time alerts:* From time to time, supplies on particular items become limited. Call accounts that use such products so they can order in advance.

10. *Follow-up to mail:* This pertains to direct-mail pieces, general correspondence, trade ads, or even invoices. Begin by informing the customer that you are just checking to see that everything was received and if there is anything you can help him with.

The critical element of meaningful calls is advance planning. TSRs must be trained to formally plan their calls, particularly in the first few months. Refer to the following sample planning form.

Exhibit 11–1

Pre-Call Planner

This form should be completed prior to each day's round of calls.
Today I am calling:

[   ] Prospective customers
[   ] Inactive customers
[   ] Active customers

My special reason [offer, sale, etc.] for calling is:

_____
_____
_____
_____
_____
_____
_____
_____
_____

I need the following information in front of me:

1. _____
2. _____
3. _____
4. _____
5. _____

I need to:

1. Establish rapport.
2. Fact-find—learn what the customer's needs are.
3. Match products with those needs.
4. Make sure customers have a current product catalog and current price list.
5. Gather all information needed to complete call report sheets.

Another element of pre-call planning is the scheduling of special sales promotions. Special promotions provide TSRs with excellent reasons to call customers and should be scheduled monthly. Use a simple Special Promotion Planner like the one in Exhibit 11–2 to keep TSRs actively involved in the promotion.

Exhibit 11–2
Special Promotion Planner

Month/year
_____

Promotional Product/Service:
_____

Probing Question(s):
_____
_____

Response/Offer/Close:
_____
_____

The blank spaces on the Special Promotion Planner for "Probing Questions" and "Response/Offer/Close" allow the telemarketing manager, through role-playing and coaching, to help TSRs develop probing questions and closes that prove to be effective. Sales promotions can be used not only as a way to entice customers, but also as a way to learn more about them. Never stop building your database on your clients.

Role-Playing Rules

Training never stops. Formal training sessions on a regular basis and daily informal or coaching sessions are essential to telemarketing success. The heart of TSR training is role-playing. To get the most out of this valuable technique, certain guidelines should be followed.

Exhibit 11–3
Call or Role-Playing Critique Form

Introduction:

Did the TSR introduce him/herself?	Yes __ No __
Was rapport established?	Yes __ No __
Did the TSR get to the business at hand?	Yes __ No __

Notes: _____

_____

Reason for call:

Did the TSR identify the decision maker?	Yes __ No __
Was a reason for the call given?	Yes __ No __
Did the TSR probe for needs?	Yes __ No __
Did the TSR find out facts needed to establish needs?	Yes __ No __

Notes: _____

_____

Sales message:

Was it delivered?	Yes __ No __
Was it persuasive?	Yes __ No __
Was it benefit-oriented?	Yes __ No __
Were objections properly managed?	Yes __ No __
Were any clues to a sale missed?	Yes __ No __
Did he/she have good product knowledge?	Yes __ No __

Notes: _____

_____

Close:

Was a trial close used?	Yes __ No __
Did the TSR close at least once?	Yes __ No __
Was it effective?	Yes __ No __
Did the TSR verify important shipping information?	Yes __ No __
Did the TSR show sincere appreciation?	Yes __ No __

Notes: _____

_____

Exhibit 11–3 (continued)
General:
Were any of the following used during the sales presentation?
[   ] Clichés [   ] Irritating repetitive phrases [   ] Negative words

Did the TSR do any of the following?
[   ] Paraphrase the prospect to indicate he/she was listening?
[   ] Listen attentively?
[   ] Recognize buying signals?

Would you have bought   [   ] Yes [   ] No   Why? _____

Additional comments:
_____
_____
_____

1. Criticism of a TSR's role-playing performance by the session leader should always be done in a positive manner.

2. The person performing the role-playing can stop at any time and ask the leader for direction.

3. No one interrupts the role-playing.

4. Everyone in the session takes notes for discussion afterwards. A critiquing form can be helpful. One that I've used in the past is reproduced here.

After every role-play encounter, the group leader should conduct a discussion among the TSRs. The person acting as the salesperson is asked such questions as:

1. Did you feel that you were consciously using telemarketing skills? If so, which ones?

2. Were you comfortable using them?

3. Which skills do you feel you used best?

4. How could you have been more effective?

The person playing the role of the customer is asked such questions as:

1. Which telemarketing skills do you think were used most effectively?

2. Did you feel you were being manipulated at any time during the conversation?

3. What portion of the presentation was most persuasive?

4. What part, if any, was flat or unconvincing?

5. Did the salesperson miss any important clues that could have led to a sale?

6. Would you have purchased from this TSR?

USING ROLE-PLAYING TO RECOGNIZE BUYING CLUES

The easiest way to explain what buying clues are is through an example. A typical buying clue occurs, for instance, when a prospect says, "I'd buy your product if it came in red." If the product comes in red, the TSR has a invitation to close the sale. But if it doesn't, the TSR has to probe to find out what it is that is so important about red and attempt to overcome the objection. All too often, TSRs miss these clues and just continue on with their prepared sales presentation. Picking up buying clues can be taught through role-playing. But the best way to teach this skill is through monitoring actual calls.

Role-Playing Customer Objections

Handling customer objections is a valuable skill that can be learned through role-playing. However, teaching it does require some preplanning on the part of the session leader. One approach is to use situation cards—one for the customer, one for the salesperson—that become the basis of role-playing (see Exhibits 11–4 and 11–5). Sets of situation cards should be made up for each of the company's products. These can be 3" × 5" typed cards that are passed out to participants or drawn from a hat. These should be designed to fit the typical sales opportunities and obstacles that TSRs face daily. They should address both specific objections and those of a more general nature.

Exhibit 11–4
Sample Situation Card

(Customer)
Play the role of a fastidious customer skeptical of everything a salesperson says. Ask for proof of product's quality. If the salesperson recognizes the type of customer you are and offers proof, order a sample.

If not, do not buy.

Exhibit 11–5
Sample Situation Card

(Salesperson)
After determining the customer's needs, begin the presentation by selling the top of the line. If the customer shows signs of being budget-conscious, promote the economy line.

FLASH CARDS

Another valuable drill for training TSRs to handle objections is the use of flash cards. Prepare a set of 8½" × 11" cards, on each of which is typed a common objection, such as:

> "It costs too much!"
>
> "Your company won't hold inventory for us!"
>
> "Our current accounting firm gets month-end figures to us within a week!"

Place a stack of the cards face down in front of each TSR, all of whom are arranged around a single table. Starting clockwise, each TSR calls out another's name and holds up the objection on the card on top of his stack. The person whose name is called must manage the objection. Afterward, other TSRs can offer alternative responses.

This is an excellent learning tool that simulates the way objections actually arise. When a TSR is confronted by an objection, there usually is not time to think or find a response in the reference guide; even computerized systems are too slow. Besides, even if a TSR does find the canned response and simply reads it, it comes across as being unnatural and unconvincing. The appropriate response should be second nature, known by heart, and delivered with feeling. Drilling with flash cards accomplishes this.

When marketing a product in a field that is dominated by a strong competitor, you often find that objections to your product or service arise in just about every sales conversation. In such cases, the TSRs should be trained to anticipate the objections *before* they are mentioned by the prospect. This approach is often referred to as the "safety blitz." The objective is to neutralize the impact of the competitor preemptively. For example:

> "Did you know our accounting firm does twice as many audits for manufacturers like yourselves as [name of competitor] does? We have even developed a special inventory control system that works on a

personal computer, which could reduce your year-end inventory adjustments to less than 1 percent, just as it has for hundreds of our other clients. Mr. Jones, who is our in-house specialist in your industry, would like to visit with you to talk about our extensive experience. Would next Tuesday at 9:00 a.m. be okay, or would Thursday at 3:00 p.m. be better?"

SALES CALL VISUALIZATION

This approach at first may seem unorthodox, but based on my experience, it works. TSRs can be taught to do a little meditation before they begin making calls each day. This is done by having them close their eyes for a few minutes and imagine or visualize in their mind's eye how the perfect call will unfold, picturing the prospects they will be calling that day. It has been found that this exercise heightens TSRs' sensitivity to prospects. They become more aware of the prospect as a person, especially his or her needs. This technique, by the way, is similar to the mental exercises used by some world-class athletes and actors before performing.

Evaluating Performance

Part of any training function is an evaluation system. TSRs learn by having their progress measured and by critiquing their own sales efforts. Figures 11–1 and 11–2 depict two evaluation reports. These can be adapted to fit your own needs. The objective of each is to have every TSR evaluate his or her own performance on a regular basis.

Motivation Techniques

Half of the telemarketing manager's job consists of preparing TSRs to make calls. The other half, however, is motivating them—keeping them interested in and excited about making calls. Enthusiasm is one of the critical parts of successful selling.

FIGURE 11–1

Weekly Project(s) Evaluations

TMC # —————————————————————————————————

Date ——————————————————————————————————

Project Title; —————————————————————————————

A. Rate the following on a scale of 1 to 4, with 1 being the lowest and 4 the highest.

Category	Score	Number, if applicable	Comments
1. Reference Guide Overview	———		———
2. Training	———		———
3. Role-Playing	———		———
4. Coaching	———		———
5. Script	———		———
6. Objection/Responses	———		———
7. Offer	———		———
8. List	———		———
9. Paperwork	———		———
10. Dialing/Hour	———	———	———
11. Comp. Calls/Hour	———	———	———
12. Orders/Hour	———	———	———

B. What held you back from maximizing your orders per hour?
   ——————————————————————————————————

C. Briefly describe your best and worst call on this project this week.
   Best: ————————————————————————————————
   ——————————————————————————————————

   Worst: ———————————————————————————————
   ——————————————————————————————————

D. What do you like and dislike about this project?
   Like: ————————————————————————————————
   Dislike: —————————————————————————————

E. How can we increase the orders per hour next week?
   ——————————————————————————————————

On the back, list any objections you did not have answers for in last week's calling.

FIGURE 11–2

Quarterly Personal Evaluation

TMC # _____

Date _____

Date of Last Evaluation _____

A. Below is a list of the projects you worked on since your last evaluation. Please rate your performance as best you can remember on a scale of 1 to 4, with 1 being the lowest and 4 being the highest, for each of the categories. After you have rated yourself, I'll add the actual number of dialings per hour, etc., and then we'll discuss the review together.

Project Description	D/Hr.*	#	CC/Hr.**	#	Ord/Hr.‡	#	Overall Rating
1.							
2.							
3.							
4.							
5.							
6.							
7.							
8.							
9.							
10.							
11.							
12.							
13.							
14.							
15.							

*D/Hr. = Dialings per hour.
**CC/Hr. = Completed calls per hour.
‡Ord/Hr. = Orders per hour.

FIGURE 11–2 (continued)

Quarterly Personal Evaluation

B. Pick 3 of the projects above and give me examples of particularly successful sales.

	Job	Example
1.	_____	_____
2.	_____	_____
3.	_____	_____

C. Pick 3 of the projects above and give me examples of lost sales.

	Job	Example
1.	_____	_____
2.	_____	_____
3.	_____	_____

D. Rate your performance over the last quarter in the following areas. Again, 1 is the lowest and 4 is the highest.

1. Establishing rapport _____
2. Creating interest _____
3. Collecting facts _____
4. Finding needs _____
5. Selling to needs _____
6. Managing objections _____
7. Closing _____
8. Paperwork _____

E. Which project did you enjoy the most? Why?

_____

_____

F. Which project did you enjoy the least? Why?

_____

_____

FIGURE 11–2 (continued)

G. What additional help or information did you need on any or all of your projects?
_____
_____

H. Did you achieve your personal goals this quarter?
_____
_____

I. Any suggestions on anything? Or any problems you'd like to discuss?
_____
_____

One important objective of motivation is to get the TSRs to achieve or exceed the sales goals they set with their telemarketing manager within the specified time frame. Consequently, TSRs must be reminded exactly what those goals are and how much they have achieved.

One way to do this is to mount a tally board on the wall of the telemarketing room. Every time a sale is made, the TSR records it on the board in a column next to the previous day's sales record. This encourages TSRs to work hard to beat the previous day's record. This approach is also used to encourage TSRs to meet weekly, as well as monthly, sales requirements. If there is more than one TSR in the center, mounting a tally board for each of them may encourage some friendly competition.

This approach also provides a basis for recognition, especially when a previous record is broken. A note from the president, an extra work break or a lunch with the boss are but a few of the customary prizes for outstanding sales performance.

PREVENTING BURNOUT

Telemarketing is extremely stressful. TSRs commonly make 30-40 sales presentations in a day and often face a rejection rate of 90 percent or more. Burnout can be an especially burdensome problem.

With a little creativity, the telemarketing manager can deal with TSR burn-out. You must keep things upbeat in the telemarketing room. Birthday celebrations become an event. Every little accomplishment should be openly commended. Criticism should be kept as positive as possible. Because of the stress of performing poorly in a telemarketing environment, it is usually unnecessary to fire a poor performer. They are driven out by the pressure.

So "fun and games" are to be taken seriously in a telemarketing environment, though they can take some strange turns. As a reward for a telemarketing sales contest, I once offered an all-expense-paid, three-day trip for two to a trade show. The lucky winner got to work 12 hours a day at our booth. Despite the schedule, it was prestigious, informative, and a nice change of pace for the winner. The contest generated excitement and enthusiasm, and the woman who won loved it. Her husband played golf the whole time.

Here is another game to try. When a sale is made or a goal reached, the lucky TSR goes to a balloon board, tosses a dart at some balloons and wins the prize described on a piece of paper inside the balloon hit by the dart. Another version of this game lets the winner draw a sealed envelope from a box that contains gift certificates. TSRs can also be divided into teams that compete for prizes or in contests in which they are given a certain sum (anywhere from a quarter to $10) on the spot for each sale made.

The object is to create excitement, not necessarily to reward. The salary and incentive programs provide rewards. Therefore, the prizes need not be elaborate. Taking the winner or winning team to lunch, giving the winner a small gift or a Friday afternoon off (which often is an inefficient time to call anyway)—these kinds of prizes work very well.

Coaching

Coaching is midway between training and motivating. Telemarketing is so stressful that it requires constant personal attention by supervisors. If this is not provided, the telephone sales operation can get out of kilter pretty quickly. The managers need to be in close enough proximity to the TSRs to overhear their conversations and to offer advice, guidance, encouragement, or criticism as necessary. It is an active and ongoing process. If managers expect success, they must be good coaches.

There's Inbound and There's Inbound Telemarketing

12

Don't confuse an inbound call with an inbound telemarketing center. Virtually all telemarketing centers make arrangements to accept some inbound calls. These may be direct, collect, or toll-free. You'd be foolish not to consider installing some toll-free lines, especially since the cost is now so reasonable—$20 per month per line, plus line time. Your outbound TSRs leave your toll-free number for hard-to-reach prospects or customers to call back. This increases the responsiveness and efficiency of your efforts.

When you do this in what is primarily an outbound center, you need to plan in advance. First, you must be able to detect when a call is inbound. One way of doing this is to assign the 800 number to one of your local lines that is seldom used, if it is not a dedicated toll-free line. For example, let's say you have a small center with three TSRs and a supervisor. Five local lines have been assigned to your people, and you are using a key-set telephone system.

When you arranged for the five local lines, you put them in a single hunt group. This means that if one line is busy, the call automatically hunts for the next available line. Therefore, if you only publish the first number in the hunt group, that's the only one the public knows about and will call. You can specify the order of the hunt. This can be set up with your local phone company after the lines are installed, if you are assigned existing lines when you go to set up telemarketing.

Normally, at any given time, two or three of your TSRs will be making outbound calls. Train them to use lines two through four, which are tied to keys 2 through 4 on the key set. Your supervisor uses line one. Assign your 800 number to ring in on line five. When line five lights up, if all the other keys are not lit, you know for sure it is an inbound call. If keys 1 through 4 are hot, the call could be either an inbound call or someone calling on the local number you publish. This isn't a foolproof system, but I've seen it work for many a small telemarketing center.

If an inbound call does come in undetected, it normally isn't a major problem. All lines are usually answered the same way. If you are in an office environment where a receptionist is available, that person can be trained to answer your inbound calls. Then he or she transfers them to the appropriate TSR or the next one available. To do this, the receptionist must have a way of identifying inbound calls. There are several ways of doing this with today's technology, besides the approach just mentioned. You need to discuss the options with your telecommunications hardware/software vendor.

I stress the importance of identifying inbound calls because these are often your most productive ones. If nothing else, the callers have returned your call out of curiosity at a time when they can talk. At best, it is someone ready to order.

As we continue with this discussion, keep in mind that basically all I've said about coaching, training, role-playing, reference guides, TSR selection, etc., holds true for inbound as well as outbound. In most cases, your objective is to sell something to someone. It may be a product, a service, an ideal, or just information. Nevertheless, people should hang up from your telemarketing center after a good, positive experience with the feeling that their call was appreciated. Always have your TSRs invite callers to call again if they can be of any further help.

An inbound telemarketing center is a center devoted solely to answering inbound calls. It is most common for these centers to be service bureaus for two reasons. First is the enormous amount of overhead required for them to be efficient. All the stations must be automated and networked. Software is required to identify to whom the inbound line is assigned when a call enters the system. It then connects the call to the proper TSR station and simultaneously pulls up the caller's account file or the information needed to successfully handle the call. All this requires a lot of programming on an ongoing basis.

Each workstation can cost anywhere from a few thousand to many thousands of dollars. A budget of $15,000 to $20,000 per station is not uncommon. The software runs from tens of thousands to hundreds of thousands of dollars. For this reason, you rarely see inbound telemarketing centers with fewer than 100 TSRs. The price tag for hardware and software can be in the millions. Smaller centers are not economical, because you must spread these high fixed costs over as many stations as possible. In most cases, there is little difference in the cost of software to handle 150 or 200 stations.

Stemming from this economic reality is the second reason most inbound centers are service bureaus. I'm referring to the volume of inbound calls required to keep 100, 200, or 500 TSRs busy or at least cost-effective. An inbound center with 200 stations can deal with an average of 25,000 calls daily, 365 days a year, 24 hours a day. How many companies generate that much daily volume?

Having to be staffed 24 hours a day can be another stumbling block for most firms. If, for example, you are a retailer hoping to generate a large response from a television commercial, when would you air it? Prime time, of course. Calls will be hot and heavy immediately following the spots and then will trickle in for hours, sometimes days. Plug in the four time zones in the United States and you start to get a feel for the challenge.

Another big thrill is trying to guess how many lines you'll need to capture 80 percent, 90 percent, or 100 percent of the calls on the caller's first attempt. Keep in mind that you lose sales if customers get busy signals. This is referred to as a blocked call. Studies indicate that most people will make only one or two attempts at most, and a good percentage only one. Each blocked call is a lost opportunity.

Since most of the calls from a TV spot are made within the first hour or so, you must be seriously overstaffed to handle this rush, compared to the rest of the time the center is open. Again, this is another reason mass merchandisers often utilize inbound service bureaus.

There are exceptions, of course—catalog marketers being one of the most prominent. They have a group of loyal customers familiar with their published business hours. A typical inbound center of this sort will have 25 to 50 TSRs. Again, sophisticated software is a basic requirement to track orders and provide the highest-quality service.

Projects ideal for the large inbound service bureaus are those requiring a minimum of technical expertise in the product or service represented. A good example would be ads that give an 800 number to call to learn the location of the nearest dealer. The TSR asks for the caller's ZIP code, and the address of the nearest location pops up on his/her screen. Another example is promotions that offer a toll-free number to get more information or a booklet of some sort. The TSR captures the name, address, and phone number of the caller, which is forwarded to advertisers. It is not uncommon for these service bureaus to handle fulfillment as well. This means the bureau mails out the requested information to the caller.

It is important to keep in mind that inbound telemarketing, unlike its outbound counterpart, relies on media other than itself to bring about action. Such media include magazine ads, radio or television commercials, direct-mail pieces, and outdoor advertising. The activity level of inbound telemarketing is directly related to the advertising media used and the markets they serve, plus the strengths and weaknesses of the advertisements.

Another important aspect of inbound telemarketing is the issue of credit card fraud. Some hints for dealing with this growing problem are presented in Appendix 5.

The Selling Mode

The primary objective of most inbound and outbound telemarketing is the same: to sell. Or, at the very least, to learn enough about potential customers to qualify them as poor, good, or hot prospects.

What are the primary differences between inbound and outbound telemarketing efforts? The two most significant are the origination of the call and the attitude of the caller.

In inbound telemarketing, the customer or prospect initiates the call and, therefore, is motivated to make the transaction. His or her level of interest in the product is high. In this respect, the customary roles of the telemarketer and the customer are reversed. However, this is not to imply that TSRs who take inbound calls should be passive listeners or simple order-takers. They must turn what may be merely an expression of interest into a firm commitment.

Of course, in those inbound telemarketing centers that are primarily order-taking operations, TSRs do not need the extensive sales training of their counterparts in outbound centers. Nor do they require as many incentives, since their function is principally reactive rather than proactive and they deal with less rejection. Nevertheless, they still need close supervision and monitoring to maintain high standards.

Qualifying Callers

One of the preeminent qualifications for a TSR in inbound telemarketing is the ability to quickly and accurately screen and qualify callers.

Although the selection of media often helps qualify callers, not all prospects are completely convinced they want to buy the product or service being offered. In fact, it is inevitable that some unqualified prospects will call. TSRs must be trained to actively screen prospects by probing—by asking questions that often are variations of the same probes used by outbound TSRs (see Chapter 11). To encourage and monitor this process, the use of an inbound call report form is highly recommended. An example is provided in Figure 12–1.

Unqualified prospects cost telemarketers time and money. One way to avoid them is to offer clear and helpful information about the product or service being offered. For example, a booklet providing a detailed description of the product or service might be offered through a toll-free number, advertised as follows:

Call 1-800-599-2001
For a Free Booklet
on
How Apex Manufacturing
Can Help You Find
the
Right System for
Your Business

FIGURE 12–1

Sample Inbound Call Report

Date _____

TSR's Initials _____

Hello, this is _____ with Apex
Manufacturing. Thank you for calling us. How may I help you?
[If they ask you for the "Right System" booklet, proceed as follows.]

1. I'll be happy to send it to you. May I have your name and address,
   please?

   Name _____
   Firm name _____
   Address _____
   City _____
   State _____ ZIP _____
   Phone [Area code first] (_____) _____

2. Where did you see the booklet advertised? _____

   [Probe to learn the specifics of the advertising media in which the
   ad was seen—the issue, date, or cover subject.]
3. Tell me a little about your specific application. _____
   _____
   _____

4. Are you currently using a product like ours? _____
5. Who are you buying from now? _____
6. What do you think of their product? _____
   _____

   [If they express any displeasure, probe those areas. Our biggest
   competitor, Acme Mfg., has a reputation for slow delivery. If they
   mention Acme, ask: "Have you ever had any delivery problems?]

FIGURE 12-1 (continued)

---

7. What kind of volume would you be considering over the next 12 months? _____

8. Is there any special information you need that I could send you now along with the free booklet? _____

[Probe for specific needs]

Thank you very much for calling Apex. I believe we can be of help to you. [Give a benefit that satisfies an expressed need—for example, "Our delivery record is the best in the industry. None of our customers has ever had to shut down an assembly line because of late delivery of our components."]

After you have had a chance to look over the free booklet, one of our salespeople will call you to see if you have any additional questions. But please don't hesitate to call us first.

Thanks again and have a good day!

A couple of pointers on how the 800 number appears in an ad or promotion are appropriate at this point. First, avoid putting the 800 portion of the number in parentheses; a quick glance can give the impression that 800 is a working area code and not a toll-free number. For instance, 801 is Utah, 802 is Vermont.

Second, businesses often select toll-free numbers that spell out the company name or some other promotional word or phrase. These are often referred to as vanity numbers. There is nothing wrong with this, as long as the number is displayed in digits as well as in letters. Ever since the numeric code became the conventional format for phone numbers, people find it difficult to dial a phone number using letters. In addition, many less expensive phones do not include letters on the dial.

FIGURE 12–2

Sample Inbound Order Form

TSR: _____

Date: _____

Shift: [If 24-hour operation] _____

Thank you for calling "The Response Center." This is _____ .
May I help you?

Catalog Page	Item	Description	Color	Size	Qty	Unit Price	Ship-ping	Total

What credit card will you be using—Visa, MasterCard, Diner's Club, or American Express? [Circle one]

Your card number: _____ Exp. date _____

BIN # _____ Issuing Bank _____

Today we have available a special offer not included in our catalog: a pair of Waterford Crystal champagne glasses. An ideal gift that we can now offer you for the price of $32.50 for the pair, a 20% discount from our normal retail price. Would you like a pair added to your order?

Will this order be shipped to you or is this a gift shipment?

Billing Name _____

Address _____

City _____ State _____ ZIP _____

Shipping Name _____

[If different from billing]

Address _____

City _____ State _____ ZIP _____

May I have your telephone number in case we have any questions about your order?

[Area Code First]   (_____) _____

183

Planning for Inbound Telemarketing

If you can furnish estimates of the expected average length of calls, the time of day most calls will be received, and the states from which the calls will come so they can be analyzed by time zones, long-distance vendors like AT&T have computer programs to determine the number of lines required.

You'll need to plan for the peak-load periods. Studies have shown that 17 percent of the calls received during a normal day occur during a single hour. It may be necessary to provide for a sufficient number of lines to handle these peaks. How many lines are necessary will depend largely on what value—or loss of value, in this case—you place on blocked calls. This simple financial decision can be made by having the TSRs keep a detailed log in which they record every incoming call and analyze the results (see Figure 12–2). Are the calls service- or sales-related? How long do the calls last? What percentage of calls result in sales? What is the average dollar value of each sale? And so on.

Your line vendor can also help in the decision by recording the number of blocked calls and displaying it on your monthly phone bill. This should be watched carefully. If there are many blocked calls or the number of blocked calls each month begins to rise, you should evaluate what they are worth in terms of lost profits. In contrast, if there are no blocked calls, or just a few, you may have too many lines and can consider canceling some.

Establishing hours for accepting calls demands careful forethought. Keeping the lines open from 8:00 a.m. to 8:00 p.m. from coast to coast would require two shifts of operators. Naturally, the hours that calls are accepted should match as closely as possible the business hours or buying habits of the targeted customer groups.

High-volume users with transcontinental sales offices have the option of redirecting calls from one sales office to another at different times of the day. For example, a line could be programmed to ring in the Chicago office after the New York office closes for the day. After Chicago closes, calls could be automati-

FIGURE 12–3

Sample Inbound Call Tracking Log

TSR _____

Date _____

Name _____

	Orders	Info Requests	Ques-tions	Call-backs	Service	Other	Total
A.M.							
07:00 – 07:30							
07:30 – 08:00							
08:00 – 08:30							
08:30 – 09:00							
09:00 – 09:30							
09:30 – 10:00							
10:00 – 10:30							
10:30 – 11:00							
11:00 – 11:30							
11:30 – 12:00							
P.M.							
12:00 – 12:30							
12:30 – 01:00							
01:00 – 01:30							
01:30 – 02:00							
02:00 – 02:30							
02:30 – 03:00							
03:00 – 03:30							
03:30 – 04:00							
04:00 – 04:30							
04:30 – 05:00							

cally redirected to Denver and then Los Angeles. Those who do not have sales offices nationwide or do not expect many calls after hours can, of course, use an answering service or machine.

ESTIMATING INBOUND LINE REQUIREMENTS

For outbound centers, the inbound line requirements are relatively easy to establish: one inbound line for every 25 TSRs is the rule of thumb.

In centers that offer inbound service only, two lines are recommended for every three TSRs, as a rule. Of course, this might not hold true for all centers, since variations in load factors and the length of the average call could make other arrangements necessary. Earlier I discussed the use of automatic attendants that answer and direct calls. These devices can also affect the number of operators required.

A careful analysis of customer buying habits will yield a more accurate estimate of how many inbound toll-free lines are needed. How often is a particular customer expected to call? Do the customer's calls tend to be long or brief?

Clearly, the hardest part of calculating inbound line requirements is anticipating how effective the advertising or promotion will be that prompts the calls. Statistics show that approximately 42 percent of all calls will come on the first day after an ad or commercial runs; approximately 36 percent on the second day; and 17 percent on the third day. The remaining 5 percent will trickle in over the active life of the particular medium used.

Example:
5,000 total inbound calls are anticipated from a magazine ad.
Day #1 = 2,100
Peak hour = 357
Day #2 = 1,800
Day #3 = 850
The remaining 250 calls would trickle in slowly over several weeks.

In this example, the center would have to be ready to handle the peak hour of the peak day—357 calls (17 percent of 2,100 calls). Assuming that each call lasts one-half minute, on average, total peak call time would be 178.5 minutes (0.5 minutes × 357 calls), which is equivalent to almost three line hours (178.5 ÷ 60 minutes = 2.975 line hours) or, more appropriately, a total of t hree inbound lines, all of which are operating for the peak hour. At least four operators would be required to cover the three inbound lines for the peak hour.

Most important, it is imperative, when determining how many lines are needed to handle inbound activity, to listen to customers. If they complain about being unable to get through, it may be time to add more lines. This, coupled with checking phone bills each month for blocked calls, should provide sufficient information for determining line capacity.

SHOULD THE INBOUND AND OUTBOUND STATIONS BE COMBINED OR SEPARATED?

In small centers, there may be no choice. But optimally, the decision should be determined by the nature and requirements of the program.

Full Account Management
Here TSRs must both sell and take care of all account-related problems, including handling inbound queries from customers. Therefore, the functions should be combined.

Outbound Sales Only
Inbound calls interrupt the rhythm of the TSRs. This is especially true if the inbound calls at a particular time deal with a different product or service from the one being sold by the outbound TSR. They should be separated, or, alternatively, all inbound calls should be funneled to a single TSR.

FIGURE 12–4

Script/Call Report for Receiving Incoming Calls From "Free Booklet" Ad in *Telemarketing Magazine* Offering

Date _____

Source _____

TM # _____

The caller will request a copy of our free booklet titled "What You Must Know BEFORE You Get into Telemarketing." So the first thing we will do is introduce ourselves and take the caller's name and address.

Hello, this is _____ with McCafferty & Associates. May I help you? We would be happy to send you that booklet. May I have your name, please?

Firm Name _____

Person's Name _____

Title _____

Address _____

City _____

State _____ ZIP _____

Phone (____) _____

[Probe to find out if they are prospects for any of our services.]

Are you currently doing any telemarketing? In-house? Using an agency? Now? Future? _____

_____

_____

Can you tell me a little about your main products?

How are they marketed? Salesman? Direct response?

_____

_____

_____

_____

_____

FIGURE 12–4 (continued)

What questions about our company can I answer for you?

_____

_____

_____

Thanks for requesting our booklet. I'm sure you'll find it a big help. If we
can be of any further help, just give us a call at our toll-free number.

_____

_____

_____

900 Numbers

A variation of the 800 toll-free number is the 900 number. The
difference is that the cost of the call is charged to the phone on
which the call is made. Since its introduction in 1981, 900 calling
has grown to a $1 billion-a-year business.

From the start, marketers loved it. They promoted all sorts of
services and products and felt assured there would never be any
payment problems, since the telephone company could cut off
service if the monthly phone bill wasn't paid. Unfortunately, it
hasn't worked out as smoothly. You've no doubt read about ado-
lescents running up fantastic bills calling sex-oriented services,
widows fleeced by fraudulent sweepstakes, or all the credit card
scams. It got to the point where the phone companies refused to
pressure patrons to pay many of the questionable services. They
also began to place stiff restrictions on the type of service permitted.

Congress responded by enacting the Telephone Disclosure and
Dispute Resolution Act. The authority for enforcing this law is
divided between the Federal Trade Commission (FTC) and the
Federal Communications Commission (FCC). The FTC passed a
regulation requiring a warning at the start of each 900 call detail-

ing the fee to be charged and giving the caller time to disconnect. Additionally, telephone companies must block calls to 900 numbers at the request of customers and all advertisements must detail all fees. Naturally, the 900 industry is lobbying against these regulations. Will they be successful? I don't know, but the forces of consumerism are very strong, as we mentioned in our discussion of the Telephone Consumer Protection Act in the Preface.

Does this mean you should give up on 900 numbers as a source of inbound telemarketing income? No, definitely not. You can get your share of this $1 billion market with a good idea. However, the trend is telling you to be careful. To be reasonable. To give your customers value for their money. Create a service that you would have no problem explaining to the gang from "60 Minutes." But then again, this should always be your policy.

Insights into Teleresearch

13

Teleresearch is the process of conducting market surveys and other types of research by phone. It is not my intention in this chapter to teach the methodology of market research, but rather to provide insights into the strengths and weaknesses of teleresearch and suggest ways of avoiding some of the regularly encountered pitfalls.

The Advantages of Teleresearch

The phone provides a fast means of performing research, since the results are available the same day the calls are made. It is subject to none of the delays associated with mail surveys—namely printing, mailing, delivery, and waiting for returns. Teleresearch is also more flexible. Once a written survey is mailed, for example, it cannot easily be changed. Researchers commonly face the problem of misinterpretation of questions by recipients. Often a slight rewording of a question makes all the difference. In teleresearch, questions can be tested by monitoring the first few calls, and if necessary, appropriate corrections can be quickly made. Teleresearch is an excellent and inexpensive way to debug a mail questionnaire before it is printed.

Another advantage of teleresearch is that the interviewer can probe the subject's initial answers to clarify something that is unclear or to encourage the respondent to talk about those areas that are especially important. Teleresearch is also particularly useful when there is a some fuzziness about the question to be researched. For instance, a company may have hundreds of satisfied customers who know and trust its existing products. Teleresearch could help it find what other products or services they need.

Teleresearch is proactive. It can elicit responses from people who often will not answer written surveys. Finally, teleresearch calls can be quickly routed to the appropriate parties in the event that the call reaches an unqualified prospect. Direct-mail surveys, once addressed, are less certain of finding the intended recipient, if he or she has moved or changed jobs. A trained TSR will find the subject or his or her replacement.

The Disadvantages of Teleresearch

The information received from a phone survey is spontaneous. The respondents are not given much of an opportunity to think through—to write and rewrite—their answers. The caller gets exactly what first comes to the subject's mind. This may be what is desired in certain kinds of research, but in other situations the researchers may want a more deliberate response. If this is true, telemarketing would be an inappropriate approach.

Because teleresearch interviews often produce "off-handed"

responses, the quality of the research findings can be disappointing. Quantitative data, particularly, may be incomplete or inaccurate. Telephone calls come unexpectedly, so respondents have no time to prepare answers or to check data. Further, people tend to be somewhat less committed to answers they provide over the phone than to answers given in person or in writing.

The casual nature of a phone call will sometimes cause people to think their answers are less confidential than they would be on a written questionnaire. They may not reveal their true feelings on sensitive subjects.

Also, since teleresearch is interactive, a subject may throw a caller off track by asking his or her own questions, changing the subject, or hanging up in the middle of the interview. This can cause problems if every question on the survey must be answered for the questionnaire to be usable.

Research requires stringent statistical criteria. Therefore, teleresearch companies must go to great lengths (and expense) to avoid skewing results in favor of the types of people who stay at home. The odds simply favor this kind of person being available when teleresearchers make their calls. Therefore, the most active types of people in our society—young singles, business professionals, and the like—often are not adequately represented in teleresearch results.

A lively or enthusiastic interviewer also can influence teleresearch results. These characteristics may encourage those interviewed to respond positively about something they may not even care about, thereby compromising the validity of the research. The exact manner in which a teleresearcher asks questions on each call can become an issue. Good telephone salespeople are taught to vary their word patterns to avoid a "sing-song" rhythm as they repeat their sales script over and over. In teleresearch, this practice could produce unreliable results. Close supervision and monitoring of teleresearchers during calls can correct this if it threatens to interfere with survey results.

Since the telephone interviewers cannot see the respondents, they miss clues that would suggest the subject is not answering thoughtfully or accurately or is not taking the questions seriously. All survey methods, of course, have a problem with deliberate misinformation, but it is particularly hard to detect in teleresearch.

Finally, long surveys are at a severe disadvantage in teleresearch. It is difficult to keep people on the phone for more than three minutes at a time, even when they are interested in the subject. Teleresearch questionnaires usually are restricted to no more than 20 questions.

Costs and Timing

The cost of conducting a teleresearch survey is an important consideration. Teleresearch usually is more expensive per completed questionnaire than mail surveys. When budgeting a teleresearch survey, the researcher's online phone time is the major cost factor. It must be taken into account when deciding how many questions to ask and how much probing the teleresearchers are to undertake on each call.

When budgeting a survey, time yourself by reading the questionnaire aloud. Quadruple the number of minutes it took you to read the questionnaire to account for dialing, waiting for an answer, bad numbers, paperwork, and so forth. Then divide this figure into 60 to arrive at an estimate of the maximum number of surveys that can be completed in an hour.

One of the key considerations is the list. The accessibility of the people on the list will significantly affect the number of surveys that can be completed per hour. It's a good idea to test a dozen or so names before finalizing the budget. It's also a good idea to have on hand three or four times the number of names that are actually needed to complete the survey, particularly if the research is needed quickly and there is no time to make callbacks to unanswered calls.

Certain research projects require statistically valid results. To get them, the sample of people surveyed must be representative of the entire population being measured. Surveys of this nature, like political polls, call for statistically valid lists. There are list companies (see Appendix 1) that specialize in providing such lists. Additionally, your TSRs may be able to speak only with certain individuals in each household. All these restraints increase costs. Be sure to plan carefully in advance.

Structuring Questions

Clearly, teleresearch works best when speed is critical and subjective information is more important than statistically significant data. But no matter what the purpose or time frame of the survey, it is crucial that research objectives be well-defined in advance so that the survey questions can be constructed accordingly.

Both open-ended and closed-ended questions can be used effectively in teleresearch. Open ended probes encourage the respondent to talk. They are equivalent to asking essay questions on a mail survey. Closed-ended questions require a yes or no, or offer multiple-choice responses. (See Exhibit 13–1.)

If the results of the survey are to be quantified, only closed-ended questions can be asked. If the goal, however, is to gain insights into a specific market or about a specific marketing problem, open-ended questions are more useful, but the answers are harder to tally, analyze, and quantify. Some researchers tape these types of surveys for transcription. Examples of both types of questions can be found later in this chapter.

Most professionally prepared surveys a use combination of open- and closed-ended questions. In these situations, the closed-ended questions are used to determine if the respondent is qualified to answer the survey, to create interest, and to obtain a specific body of required information. Open-ended questions are usually used at the beginning and/or end of the survey.

EXHIBIT 13–1

Examples of Closed-Ended Questions:

1. Does your family currently own a videocassette recorder?

   [   ] Yes   [   ] No

   If yes: Go to question #2.
   If no: Do you plan on buying one in the next six months?

   [   ] Yes   [   ] No

2. How many television sets are there in your home at this time?

   Number _____

Multiple-choice questions for teleresearch could be structured as follows:

I'm going to read you a list of features of our most popular sports car. Tell me if you consider these features very important, somewhat important, or not important at all.

	Very	Somewhat	Not at All
1. It has a sun roof.	x	x	x
2. It can accelerate to 50 mph in 6.5 seconds.	x	x	x
3. A stereo radio/cassette player is standard.	x	x	x
4. It sells for under $25,000.	x	x	x

[The interviewer circles the response.]

Examples of Open-Ended Questions:
1. What do you expect from an accounting firm?
2. What specific problems have the recent revisions to the tax code caused your company?
3. How do you plan to address them?

The simplest, least threatening questions should be asked first. This builds a certain amount of trust and confidence in the respondent. People become embarrassed when they cannot answer the first question asked. If the survey sounds difficult in the beginning, respondents often refuse to continue rather than risk appearing foolish.

A great deal of planning should be should be done on the information being requested and the wording of the questions. The closer questions are to people's personal lives, livelihoods, or income levels, the lower the response rate you can expect.

We all have a tendency to resist answering personal questions asked by strangers. If information about income or age is requested, for example, it should be asked near the end of the survey. It often helps to defuse personal questions by only asking for ranges; for instance, "Which age group are you in—55 to 64, 64 to 74, or over 74?" This method usually provides information that is just as valuable as more exact answers.

The accompanying sample questionnaire was written for an accounting firm that specializes in servicing midsized manufacturing firms. The objective was to screen a list of prospects to uncover the most promising leads.

Notice the opening. Little or no reason for the survey is given. An explanation is unnecessary in most cases; it is best to jump right into the questions. Explanations often stimulate the subjects to ask questions of their own.

Never underestimate the amount of confidential information you can get over the phone. It is amazing, but individuals will often disclose proprietary information, such as production volume, costs and manufacturing processes, vendors' names, model numbers of the components they buy, and how long it takes them to manufacture various products.

As the questionnaire illustrates, it is important to place directions for the teleresearchers throughout the survey as signposts

EXHIBIT 13–2
Sample Questionnaire

Hello, my name is ——————— with Furthermore Research.

May I speak with the vice president of accounting?

[Capture name from receptionist; reintroduce yourself when subject answers phone.]

Hello, Mr. ——————— . My name is ———————
with Furthermore Research. I'm calling financial vice presidents, like yourself, to ask a few questions about their accounting needs. Do you have a few minutes?

[*If any hesitation:* It will only take two minutes.]

[*If no:* Can I call you back at a better time?]

[Qualify subject]

1. You are the vice president of accounting, aren't you?
   [   ] Yes   [   ] No

2. Are you the person who oversees all the accounts for your company?
   [   ] Yes   [   ] No
   [*If no:* Who does? ———————————————]

3. Does your company do all its day-to-day accounting internally?
   [   ] Yes   [   ] No

4. Is your company public or private?
   [   ] Public   [   ] Private

5. Do you retain an independent accounting firm to do an annual audit?
   [   ] Yes   [   ] No

EXHIBIT 13–2 (continued)

6. Are you the person who selects that firm?
    [   ] Yes   [   ] No
    [*If no:* Who makes the selection? _____]

7. Do you use the same firm each year?
    [   ] Yes   [   ] No

8. Could you give me the name?
    [   ] No   [   ] Yes _____

9. If you had to do it over, what would you change about the way last
    year's audit was conducted? _____
    _____

    Thank you very much for your time. Have a good day.

---

and reminders. When a teleresearcher is talking on the phone and recording responses, there is precious little time to think.

Occasionally a subject will press to find out the "who and why" behind the survey. The teleresearcher must have an answer for this. A possible answer might be: "We are unable to divulge the name of our client at this time. Please feel free to refuse to answer any question you believe too confidential. The first question is . . . ."

Reaching the Right Respondent

When calling high-level corporate officers, researchers often can get information from secretaries or administrative assistants that is as good, if not better, as what can be obtained from the actual prospects. Therefore, it pays for teleresearchers to talk first to whomever they reach before making repeated callbacks. The information being sought may require that executives be surveyed, but talking to second- or third-level personnel is often a valid alternative that can save time and money. In the sample questionnaire, the vice president's executive secretary could probably provide all of the information being sought.

There are many reliable sources of various kinds of information:

- The sales departments of most companies usually are sources of general information. Talk to anybody who answers the phone in that department. Ask them to send sales literature (to your home address, if you need to maintain anonymity).

- For financial information on public companies, the public relations department is the best bet. Request copies of annual reports, 10-Ks, and quarterly financial reports.

- For more detailed information about a product, speak to chief engineers. More often than not, they will share a great deal of information as long as they are assured that the caller is not a competitor. Engineers understand the significance of research and may therefore be more disposed to cooperate.

- Purchasing agents usually are helpful in providing information on how to become an approved vendor or in areas where they are having problems finding suppliers. But since they spend so much of their working lives on the phone, they are quick to hang up.

- With small businesses, talk with the receptionists or office managers. They are often involved in several of the company's functions and can be quite communicative. Also, being surveyed makes them feel important.

- Service representatives usually are very cooperative. They are accustomed to talking on the phone and spend much of their time informing customers about their companies.

Teleresearcher Training

Of course, as in any telemarketing project, time must be devoted to training teleresearchers. Like telemarketers, they must be prepared for overcoming respondents' objections to participating in the survey. The "I have no time" objection is one of the toughest to overcome. Role-play is still the key training tool. Simulate situations involving cooperative, uncooperative, hostile, and inquisitive respondents. During surveys, listen to as many calls as possible. Check to make sure your TSRs are not influencing the answers. This is more of a problem with your best salespeople than with the others.

Spend as much time as necessary explaining the objectives of the survey. Often, incidental conversations can take place during a survey. If the TSRs know the objectives and the methodology, they are less likely to let anything interfere with getting reliable data. Also, if extraneous information offered by those being surveyed is to be captured, let your people know in advance.

Despite its restrictions, teleresearch has a legitimate place in serious research.

International
Telemarketing

14

As alluded to in the Preface, there are some incredible opportunities to sell by phone internationally. It can even be done on a modest scale.

Let me give you an example. A commodity futures brokerage firm I've worked with received inquiries from investors in Europe, particularly Germany. The question arose on how to capitalize on this interest. A call to AT&T told us a toll-free line from Germany to our Chicago office would cost only $20 per month service fee plus the online charges and a small one-time installation fee. Two weeks later, we had a direct link to our German customers and prospects. Advertising the number in several German papers helped build business.

I use this story because it illustrates some of the important points regarding international telemarketing you need to become familiar with, such as the following:

1. *The Draw:* What products or services will attract foreign buyers by country? We are selling the excitement and profit potential of trading in the U.S. futures markets. Having an office in the same building as the Chicago Mercantile Exchange further enhances the draw. When prospects call, we can conference them directly to the trading pits. Our European investors are right on the exchange floors listening to the trading frenzy that takes place at one of the world's largest and most famous futures exchanges.

   Rule One is to make sure your product or service is something foreign buyer can't easily get at home. If this has a ring of familiarity, it is because good direct marketers do not offer the same products that are readily available in retail stores. Since buyers must go out of their way, the product must be different or special in some way. Every country has certain products that attract customers from all over the world. To be successful in international direct marketing, particularly on a modest budget, it helps to have one of these products.

2. *The Language:* About two-thirds of the German investors we attracted spoke English fluently. Nevertheless, we hired German-speaking brokers to make these customers more comfortable and to improve communications.

   Rule Two is to achieve competency in the native language of the countries you wish to do business.

3. *Time Zones:* Germany is seven time zones ahead of Central Standard Time in the United States. Most Chicago exchanges trade from 8:30 a.m. to 3:15 p.m., which is 3:30 p.m.to 10:15 p.m. in central Europe. Our German investors could trade after work—a very convenient arrangement.

   Rule Three is to make sure you are open when customers want to do business.

4. *Local Laws and Customs:* This is the only real negative we ran into with Germans trading the futures markets. Their law does not enforce our rights to collect trading debts, if they lose more money than is in their trading accounts. We tried to protect ourselves by requiring a high initial investment.

Rule Four is to protect your business. Do your homework. Learn if there are any local laws that either hamper the way you normally do business or put you at unreasonable risk.

We've just discussed the value of installing a toll-free telephone line in a foreign country. You can also do this to attract business from Americans living abroad. For example, you can advertise in international editions of newspapers and magazines. Study the worldwide circulation of *The Wall Street Journal* or the *Herald Tribune*. Some major foreign newspapers print an English edition that reaches expatriates. Don't forget to request a toll-free number so you have it to put in the paper. AT&T offers the service from approximately 60 countries at the moment.

AT&T also has several other services along this line that you might find useful. They are part of AT&T's enhanced 800 service. Inbound calls can be routed to a specific extension at your call center by country. Calls from Spain go to Spanish-speaking call center representatives (TSRs). Another service provides for a recorded message available in over 100 languages. A Turk would get a recording in Turkish asking him to leave a message or provide his address and phone number to receive a catalog, a callback, or to place an order. They also have interpreters available to translate calls. Or you can advertise your toll-free number in that country's 800 directory, several of which are already in print. A little creativity might result in cracking a whole new market for your company. The international section of the Department of Commerce and your state's economic development commission can also help.

Another trick I've found that works is to run ads in foreign countries in English. The people who respond usually speak enough English to get through the conversation, or they enlist the help of someone who does. This cuts down response, but it works well enough for preliminary market testing. Is there enough interest to risk spending some serious promotional bucks?

THE INTERNATIONAL TELEMARKETING CENTER

Now, we begin thinking major investments in time and money. Should you consider an outbound telemarketing campaign internationally? This is extremely complex. With the previously discussed inbound efforts, prospects were motivated to call you for whatever reason. They knew they were calling an English-speaking business. Therefore, they were prepared to deal with the language difference, if there was one.

With outbound, you're the aggressor. You can no longer get away with sidestepping a language barrier. Additionally, you are contacting the prospects at your convenience, which means you must capture their interest. You're the aggressor!

Before attempting to launch an international outbound telemarketing campaign, answer the following questions:

1. Are telephones even available in the countries you are considering? In Mexico, one in six homes has a phone. In Brazil, the ratio is 1 to 11. In most cases in developing nations, phones are only in the homes of the upper and middle classes and larger businesses.

2. What about the quality and reliability of the local phone service? We often take the speed and clarity of our system for granted. Do some test calls just in case, if you have any doubts.

3. Will your foreign customers be able to pay you? For example, South Africans can purchase bank drafts in their

rands only up to $50 U.S. Credit cards are not available in every country. Many places in the world have severe restrictions on native currency leaving their country.

4. Keep an eye on the exchange rate. A strong U.S. dollar, compared to the currency of the country you're marketing to, makes your product more expensive to your customers. A weak one works in your favor.

5. Is your product suited for your target market? U.S. automakers have been trying to sell cars with steering wheels on the left in countries like Japan for years and wondering why they haven't caught on. It is probably for the same reason that English right-handed cars never became popular in this country.

6. Are the political winds blowing at your back or in your face? Who could get enthusiastic about selling American-made goods in Iraq or Iran these days?

7. Are there any legal restrictions you should be aware of? Some countries outright prohibit outbound telemarketing. Still others have restrictive privacy laws, such as a prohibition against storing a person's gender in your database. The EC has been working on some very restrictive regulations on how direct-marketing lists can be used. Many of the legal problems stem from countries attempting to protect their local businesses, and the regulators can get downright nasty if they decide you are trying to put natives out of business.

8. Are there any local customs you need to take into consideration? In Japan, up until recently, it was considered uncivilized to do outbound telemarketing.

9. What is perceived as quality, after-sale service? Once you make sales, the customers must be serviced. The concept of quality services varies from country to country. In financial

circles, Europe leans more toward *caveat emptor* than the United States, while in Japan, brokerage firms have been known to refund money lost in the markets to large customers. How's that for service? Therefore, you must determine what services are necessary and budget for them.

10. Does language mean more than vocabulary? It sure does. Your TSRs will need more than two years of high school French to communicate with Parisians. Most professional firms require supervisors of call center representatives to be natives of the country being contacted.

If all this scares you away, you still must decide if you should set up your own call center or hire a service bureau. I'd recommend a test **in your target country** before doing too much on your own. The exception is the inbound center discussed earlier.

The next question: where is a good location for an international telemarketing center? If your target is the 340-million-person marketplace that will someday be the European Economic Community, my preference would be Ireland as the base. It offers the following advantages:

- Competitive wage rate

- Low telcom costs servicing all of Europe

- Very competitive facility costs

- Plentiful supply of multilingual salespeople

- Strong and stable economic environment

- Financial aid programs available from its Industrial Development Authority

All this and a maximum 10 percent corporate profits tax rate! It would also be an advantage to work out of a country that speaks English, unless your management staff was multilingual. Then there are all those wonderful golf courses.

Finally, you should not overlook the potential of multilingual telemarketing right here in the U.S. of A. People, particularly immigrants, are more comfortable buying from someone who speaks their native tongue. The U.S. Census Bureau reports show that almost three out of four Hispanic adults in the this country speak only Spanish at home. This is one of the fastest-growing minorities and deserves special attention, if you have products or services its members need.

Another interesting group is the Asians, particularly the Vietnamese, Koreans, and Chinese. All of these groups are growing at a fast pace and are the least likely to be fluent in English. It's interesting to note that the average income for Vietnamese is 8 percent higher than the U.S. average. You can do plenty of "international" telemarketing without leaving this country. It is a good way to develop experience before moving overseas.

Sources for More Information

This appendix is not intended to be all-inclusive but rather to present a list of certain sources for readers who seek more detail on specific areas of telemarketing. Write to or call these sources (of course, we prefer that you call!) for catalogs or additional information.

Some Sources Mentioned in the Text

American Telemarketing Association, Inc.
5000 Van Nuys Boulevard, Suite 400
Sherman Oaks, CA 91403
800-441-3335

American Telemarketing Association, Inc.
1800 Pickwick Avenue
Glenview, IL 60025
(312) 724-7700

Consider joining, if you're serious about telemarketing.

Direct Marketing Association
Telephone Council
6 East 43rd Street
New York, NY 10017
(212) 689-4977

TELEMAGIC Software
Remote Control International
5928 Pascal Court
Carlsbad, CA 92008
(619) 431-4000
800-835-MAGIC

Call for the location of your nearest dealer to get a demo disk.

TeleDirect International, Inc.
5510 Utica Ridge Road
Davenport, IA 52807
800-531-6440

If you're telemarketing to consumers, look into TeleDirect's predictive dialing software.

Finding Facts Fast: How to Find Out What You Want to Know Immediately, by Alden Todd. New York: William Morrow & Co.

Read this book if you are completely in the dark on where to begin looking for information.

General Telemarketing Information

For information on telemarketing staffing, training, equipment, hardware, software, and budgeting. Write or call these companies for more information, catalogs, or samples.

AT&T

AT&T has a program called Knowledge Plus. It provides comprehensive, up-to-date information on all phases of phone communications, including telemarketing. Contact the local AT&T account executive or call 1-800-222-0400.

D M News
19 West 21st Street
New York, NY 10010
(212) 741-2095

This controlled-circulation weekly publication covers direct marketing with regular features on telemarketing. Its ads are excellent sources for lists to test.

Direct Marketing Magazine
224 Seventh Street
Garden City, NY 11530

Fraud & Theft Information Bureau
217 North Seacrest Boulevard
Box 400
Boynton Beach, FL 33425
(305) 737-7500

Consultants on credit card fraud.

Marketing Communications Magazine
475 Park Avenue South
New York, NY 10016

NATA's Telemarketing Source Book
P.O. Box 39989
Washington, D.C. 20016
800-538-6282
(202) 296-9800

A collection of information on equipment, software, trade shows, periodicals, etc., for telemarketers.

Telecommunications
5610 Washington Street
Dedham, MA 02026

Telehints
167 Corey Road, #111
Brookline, MA 02146

Telemarketing Magazine
Selling Techniques Newsletter
One Technology Plaza
Norwalk, CT 06854
800-243-6002
(203) 852-6800

Offers many helpful articles each month on telemarketing equipment, as well as on managing, motivating, and training TSRs. The December issue is the annual buyers' guide, which includes lists of hundreds of vendors. This may be the best source to begin shopping for telemarketing equipment and services.

TeleProfessional
209 West Fifth Street
Suite N
Waterloo, IA 50701-5420
(319) 235-4473

An excellent resource for telemarketing supervisors.

The Book on Business Phone Systems
AmeriTech Communications
300 South Riverside Plaza
Chicago, IL 60606
(312) 930-2600

The Complete Handbook of All-Purpose Telemarketing Scripts
Prentice-Hall
P.O. Box 11071
Des Moines, IA 50381-1071

The How to Buy a Phone Book
Walker Telecommunications Corporation
200 Oser Avenue
Hauppauge, NY 11788
(516) 435-1000

Crabdall Associates, Inc.
Executive Recruiters in Direct Mail & Telemarketing
114 East 32nd Street
Suite 1238
New York, NY 10016
(212) 213-1700

Publish an annual *Direct Marketing and Telemarketing National Salary Guide.* Write for a copy.

List Sources

Encyclopedia of Associations
Gale Research Company
Book Tower
Detroit, MI 48226
800-223-GALE

A listing of 19,500 national and 2,000 international organizations and 4,000 consulting firms, as well as other sources of list information. Available in the reference section of most libraries.

National Technical Information Service
U.S. Department of Commerce
Springfield, VA 22161

This organization will send you catalogs of computerized lists. These are useful if you are selling to companies that require special federal permits, such as toxic waste disposal licenses.

Standard Rate & Data Service, Inc.
Direct Mail List Rates and Data
5201 Old Orchard Road
Skokie, IL 60077

This is a directory of lists available to rent: includes thousands of possibilities.

The following are list compilers and brokers:

American Business Lists, Inc.
5707 South 86th Circle
P.O. Box 27347
Omaha, NE 68127   (402) 331-7169

Complete coverage of the telephone *Yellow Pages* on a national basis. They provide printed lists, disks (in TELEMAGIC's format), customized directories, and even direct access to their databases. Write or call for a catalog.

American Direct Marketing Services, Inc.
1261 Record Crossing
Dallas, TX 75235
800-527-5080   (214) 634-2361

They have many lists with telephone numbers.

CCX Network, Inc.
301 Industrial Boulevard
Conway, AR 72032
800-638-7378

An excellent source for names, plus worthwhile databases. This company does a lot of list enhancement.

Customized Mail Lists, Inc.
158-23 Grand Central Parkway
Jamaica Estates, NY 11432
(212) 969-8800

Dependable List Compilation
215 Northwest Highway
Barrington, IL 60010
(312) 382-4501

Dunhill International Lists Co., Inc.
2430 West Oakland Park Boulevard
Ft. Lauderdale, FL 33311
800-223-1882
(305) 484-8300

Dun's Marketing Services
Dun & Bradstreet
Three Century Drive
Parsippany, NJ 07054
(201) 455-0900

Provides credit information on its lists, as well as other demographics.

Executive Services Companies
P.O. Box 2407
Richardson, TX 75080
800-527-3933   (214) 699-1271

George-Mann Associates
6 Old Cranbury Road
Cranbury, NJ 08512
800-257-5120   (609) 443-1330

List Horizons
A Division of Compilers Plus, Inc.
Pelham Manor, NY 10803
800-431-2914   (914) 738-1520

Market Data Retrieval
16 Progress Drive
Shelton, CT 06484
800-MAIL-NOW

More than 7.5 million U.S. businesses are in this company's computerized file. Offers flexible selection criteria, such as by SIC (Standard Industrial Classification) code or number of employees.

Metromail
901 West Bond Street
Lincoln, NE 68521
(402) 475-4591

Over 7.5 million names of consumers available with geographic and demographic selections.

National Decisions Systems
Equifax, The Information Source
539 Encinitas Boulevard
Encinitas, CA 92024
800-866-6510

Business-Facts list contains over 10 million individual business locations in the United States. A comprehensive consumer list is available as well. Lists are enhanced with census data, surveys, and other data. Call for catalog.

National Farm Data Bank
131 Lincoln Highway
Frankfort, IL 60423
(815) 469-2163

One of the few sources of farmer lists with phone numbers.

Network Lists & Data, Inc.
400 Halstead Avenue
P.O. Box 327
Harrison, NY 10528
800-431-1598   (914) 835-5353

Seven million business prospects from *Yellow Pages* and trade directories. Call or write for a catalog.

Poor's Register of Corporations,
Directors and Executives
Standard & Poor's Corporation
McGraw Hill
New York, NY 10004
800-221-5277   (212) 208-8812

R. L. Polk & Co.
4850 Baumgartner Road, Suite 200
St. Louis, MO 43129
(314) 894-3590

One of the major compilers of all kinds of lists, both business and consumer.

Research Projects Corporation
Pomperpary Avenue
Woodbury, CT 06798
800-243-4360   (203) 263-0100

Edith Roman
875 Avenue of the Americas
New York, NY 10001
800-223-2194   (212) 695-3836

Survey Sampling, Inc.
180 Post Road East
Westport, CT 06880
(203) 266-7558

This is the place to consider if you need statistically valid samples. Additionally, you can select from millions of names using up to five demographic characteristics to describe a target market.

Uni-Mail Commercial
One Lincoln Plaza
New York, NY 10023
800-223-1033   (212) 580-3000

U.S. Industrial Director
Cahners Publishing Company
270 Saint Paul Street
Denver, CO 80206-9988

Worldata
5200 Town Center Circle
Boca Raton, FL 33486
800-331-8102

International Telemarketing Resources

Lavery Rowe Advertising-London
011-44-71-378-17-80

Specializes in adapting American mail-order ads to work in Europe.
Can assist with fulfillment.

Ireland Industrial Development Authority
IDA Head Office
Wilton Park House
Wilton Park
Dublin 2
Ireland
353-1-686632

Regional offices: New York City (212-972-1000), Atlanta (404-351-
8474), Boston (617-367-8225), Chicago (312-236-0222), Los Angeles
(310-829-0081), and San Jose (408-294-9903). Can provide important
incentives and information on telemarketing in Europe.

Telecom Ireland
c/o Telecom Ireland (US) Limited
Stamford, CT 06901
800-445-4475

Least expensive inbound toll-free numbers in Europe. Digital link to
the United States. Multilingual work force and call center facilities
available.

Tele-Direct
DMF Direct Marketing France
97, rue Jean-Jaures
92300 Levallois Perret
France
011-33-1-47-39-00-44

Provides inbound and outbound telemarketing.

Presto Worldwide, Inc.
P.O. Box 148
Aldie, VA 22001
(703) 327-2603

Lists from all over the world—Europe, Pacific Rim, Latin America—40 countries available.

Schober Direkmarketing, Inc.
206 West 15th Street
New York, NY 10011
(212) 691-8869

Over 40 million business names and nearly 1 billion consumer names available worldwide.

Inter Europe
Wilhelminapark 6
NL-2012 KA Haarlem
Netherlands
31-23-319-129

Provides direct mail and multilingual telemarketing throughout Europe. U.S. sales representative can be reached at (304) 947-7368.

THE
REFERENCE
GUIDE

A workbook and training manual
containing all the material you need to successfully
sell over the telephone.

Learn How to Sell
into Your Customer Needs

McCafferty & Associates
2323 Loma Street
Cedar Falls, IA 50613

Table of Contents

Guide Section

Workbook Section

I. Introduction

Telephone sales or telemarketing, as it is most commonly called, is the planned use of the telephone in conjunction with all the other marketing, advertising, and selling your organization currently does.

The key words are "planned" and "in conjunction with."

The function of this Reference Guide is to assist you in preparing and organizing all the material you need in front of you when you are on the phone selling. It is designed to be used on a TeleEasel. (See illustration below.)

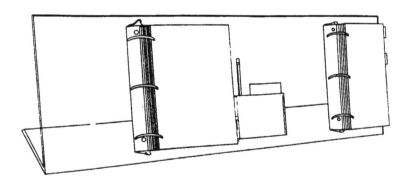

If you don't have a TeleEasel, you may substitute a three-ring easel binder, or use it flat like a deck of flip cards. No matter how you use it, the Reference Guide will improve the quality of every inbound or outbound call.

II. How to Use

1. Read through the entire Reference Guide first to become completely familiar with it.

2. Select those areas that are pertinent to your company's products or services. Complete the directions specified in each section. You may want to write your notes first on a scratch pad and then copy them neatly or have them typed on the permanent cards. Remember, you're going to have to be able to read the information under the pressure of a call.

   In some cases, you may want to get your supervisor's approval and participation.

   If you are one of a group of telephone sales representatives, consider working as a team and selecting the best ideas from the group. It is important that everyone on the phone give the same information to your customers and prospects.

3. Next, begin training with the Reference Guide. Read and discuss the Telephone Sales Techniques. You should spend at least four hours on this section the first day. On all subsequent sales days, you should spend 10-15 minutes reviewing pertinent sections, either on your own or as a group.

   Each morning ask yourself these questions:

- What did I forget to do the last time I was on the phone?

- Did I use open probes?

- Did I find a customer's need?

- Did I use any negative words?

- Which positive words did I use?

- Did I ask meaningful questions?

- Was I talking too fast or too slow?

- How well did I listen?

- Did I pick up on the customer's buying signals?

- Was I pleasant, fun to talk with?

- Would the people on the other end of the line describe me as helpful, sincere, confident, reliable, intelligent, aloof, mechanical, or uninformed?

- Did I overcome objections?

Your objective on each call is twofold. You must help the company you work for by selling its products or services. You must also help your customers and prospects find out how your company's products or services can solve their problems or help them do their work easier, faster, or at a lower cost. Professional selling is a two-way street.

4. The key to learning how to sell over the phone is role-playing. Select a partner. Take turns playing the role of

a telemarketer calling an active customer, inactive customer, prospect, or whomever your target market is.

Have your partner play the part of a satisfied, unsatisfied, cooperative, belligerent, well-informed, and ignorant customer or prospect. Get a feel for the facts you will need to handle and the different types of calls you'll encounter.

5. Make a preliminary string of test calls. Find out what the real world is like. Use what you learn to make modifications, corrections, changes, and refinements to your Reference Guide. Do this in cooperation with the other telephone service reps and your supervisor. The Reference Guide should be a living, growing, changing tool.

6. Develop a set routine to follow every day. Allow time for review and preparation, actual calls, breaks, and follow-up. A typical day could look like this:

9:00 - 9:15   Review. Role-playing.

9:15 - 9:30   Preparation. Looking up phone numbers.

9:30 - 12:00   Calls (with one 15-minute break).

12:00 - 12:30   Lunch

12:30 - 12:45   Preparation. Review morning's calls.

12:45 - 3:30   Calls (with one 15-minute break).

3:30 - 5:00   Paperwork. Solve problems for
               tomorrow's callbacks, obtain answers
               to questions, check customer
               invoices, etc.

Developing a routine that works depends on the type of persons you are calling and when they can be reached. With the schedule above, five hours are spent on the phone. In that period of time, you should be able to make approximately 25 to 50 good person-to-person sales presentations.

III.   Selling by the Phone

There are several ways of making sales using the phone. The first, of course, is just brute strength. It's called canvassing. You simply call as many prospects as you can, as fast as you can, telling them what you're selling and asking for an order.

This works for some products, like tickets to sports events— particularly if there is a limited supply of tickets and a virtually unlimited supply of sports fans. Eventually, you're going to stumble across enough people who want to go to the game.

A variation of this is called "Smile'n'Dial." Here, again, you're playing the numbers game and trying to reach as many prospects as possible. The difference is you're using a prepared script that goes into more detail about whatever you're selling. The prospect is at least made aware of some reasons for buying.

Again, this can work, but the recipients of the calls don't actively participate in the call. They are read a script and asked to make a decision. If the script hits a nerve, a sale is made.

These first two types of sales calls can work for one-time sales to an unlimited audience. If you're after repeat business or have a limited number of prospects, you should develop what we call the Need Sale.

The most successful sales occur when you uncover an honest need your customer or prospect has, and then demonstrate how the product or service you're selling satisfies that need.

At first, this appears to be a more difficult sale, but it really isn't. It does take a little more work on your part to learn about your products and your customers' needs.

But it actually becomes an easier call because you're more involved in the calls. All calls are not exactly alike. You're asking questions. Sharing information. Helping people solve problems. The tough calls are the ones you have to do over and over and over again. Exactly the same way each time at breakneck speed.

This Reference Guide contains all the information you need to know to successfully make Need Sales on the phone.

IV. Telephone Selling Fundamentals

Your voice is your personality when you're on the phone. The people you talk to can tell when you're smiling, happy to be talking to them. More important, they can tell when you don't want to talk to them.

The telephone is as important to the sales department as the calculator is to accounting. More often than not, when a business loses customers, it's because the lines of communication break down.

If you have a good talking relationship with your customers, you can overcome a multitude of problems and misunderstandings. The best part is that they become better and better customers each day.

So don't take your telephone manners for granted. Work on them each day.

Here are some important tips:

1. Don't eat, chew gum, or smoke when you're on the phone.

2. Psyche yourself up so that each time you pick up the phone you have a smile in your voice.

3. On incoming calls, always try to answer on the first or second ring.

4. Sing out your greeting! Let the person on the other end of the line know you're alert, alive, and ready to do business.

5. Start each call by identifying yourself. Always let the people know to whom they are speaking: "This is Joan with Ace Manufacturing!"

6. Ask questions. Let your prospects/customers know you're interested in them.

7. Don't dominate the conversation. You can control the course of a call better by asking the right questions. Don't try to overpower the person you're speaking with.

8. Keep a business attitude. Establish a friendly relationship but don't spend a lot of time with small talk. Always remember, you're calling on serious business.

9. Develop good listening skills. Plan your calls in advance and have all the information you'll need in front of you so you're not furiously trying to think of what to say next. Sit back and listen.

10. Learn at least one thing from each call. After each call, you should know a little more about your target audience—and even a little more about yourself.

11. Think like your customer. Try to put everything you say in the context of your customer's position.

12. Don't interrupt. It's rude, and it tells your customers that whatever you have to say is more important than what they have to say.

13. Hear them out. If you assume you know what they are going to say, you'll be unpleasantly surprised all too often. Avoid completing sentences mentally or verbally.

14. Keep your mind open. Sales conversations often go in strange directions leading to unexpected opportunities. Listen for them.

15. Don't rely on your memory. Become an ardent note taker, if you're not already.

16. Isolate what's important. Pick out the clues you hear that will lead to a sale. Discard the meaningless chit-chat.

17. Look your caller "straight in the eye." Pay attention, just like you would if you were face-to-face. Block out all the noise and commotion around you.

18. Let them know you're still listening. Say "Yes, I see" or "You know, you're right" or at least an occasional "Uh-huh!"

19. Concentrate on *what* is being said, not how. React to the ideas you're hearing, not how the person sounds.

20. Think about selling. A good string of sales will take all your worries away.

21. Avoid arguing, even mentally.

22. Stay awake, mentally and physically. Ever consider how loud a yawn can be over the phone?

23. Be yourself. Let your nature express itself.

24. Simplify everything. Use small words. Build complex ideas one piece at a time.

25. Create verbal excitement. A monotone voice puts listeners to sleep. Use your voice to instill excitement!

26. Use the King's English. Try not to slur your words. Speak distinctly. Avoid slang.

27. No accents allowed. If you have a strong regional accent, work at minimizing its effect. The only exception is if it fits your product. For example, if you're selling Deep South Frozen Pecan Pies, go ahead and sound like you were born in the "Heart of Dixie."

28. Watch the bull! Tall tales are great at a liar's convention, but you must always maintain your credibility when selling. Avoid exaggerated claims.

29. Feel the part you're playing. Learn your sales presentation so well you can discard the script.

30. Always be a lady or a gentleman. Remember what Mom said: "You can catch more flies with sugar than with vinegar." Courtesy still pays, especially in telephone sales.

31. The first one done doesn't necessarily win. Be sensitive to the pace of the conversation. Don't hurry. Don't delay.

32. Hedgers lose. Answer questions directly. Don't beat around the bush. If you don't know the answer, say so. Tell them you'll get the correct answer and call back.

33. Even more important, don't fake it. You'll get caught if you do.

34. Try not to be dumb twice. Once you get an answer to a tough question, add it to your Reference Guide by writing it on one of the blank pages provided.

35. Hogs are lonely. Share the answers to tough questions with your colleagues.

36. Become a Rembrandt on the phone. Paint word pictures. Help your prospects to visualize what your products are and how they can satisfy their needs.

37. Sell the sizzle, not the steak. Talk about how your product can make money for your customers or save time or make life easier. Don't just tell them it's red, weighs 50 pounds, and belongs in everybody's garage.

38. Press for specifics. Make sure you get specific answers to the questions you ask. A casual, general answer may not do you any good.

39. Avoid callbacks whenever possible. Plan your calls carefully—especially the answers to likely questions, so you don't have to make expensive and needless return calls.

40. Feedback is important information. When you repeat critical data to the customer, you double-check that you understand the facts exactly.

41. Show them you care. Remember or take notes about personal items and ask about them when you call. "How was your vacation?" This builds rapport.

42. Don't be bashful. If you don't understand something, ask. There's nothing people like more than to demonstrate their intelligence. Learn to make this human characteristic work for you.

43. Avoid the butterfly syndrome. Stick to your subject. Don't fly from one idea to the other.

44. Don't promise the moon. We all want to please others, but if you give away more than you're authorized, you'll have to make an embarrassing callback to tell your customer he can't have what you promised.

45. Verify important details. At the end of each call, double-check the spelling of names, addresses, and, most important, what was ordered. Leave nothing to chance.

46. Think tracking. Have definite plans before you get on the phone to keep track of prospects or customers who may require a callback.

47. Set goals. Learn in advance what your company and supervisor expect from each day's calls. Then set your own personal goals.

48. Eliminate duplicate calls. Devise a system so that duplicate listings from different sources can be avoided as much as possible. It's a waste of time and money for two people to call the same prospect—not to mention the fact that it makes your firm appear disorganized.

49. Always walk away from winning hands. Take your break or end your day on a positive call. This gives you a running start on your next series of calls.

50. The odds are always in favor of the house. Sales come to those who persevere. Dial your way through slumps; we all have them from time to time.

Add your own rules here:

V. Special Selling Skills

1. *Selling into your customer's needs.*

This is probably the most useful skill any salesperson can develop. You may even find it handy in your personal life.

Like most really helpful behavior patterns, it is easy to learn but requires a lot of discipline and practice. All it entails is uncovering the needs of the person you're talking to. This is done by asking questions and listening for clues.

Open-ended questions are those that cannot be answered with a one- or two-word answer. Here are two questions you might ask your baby sitter tonight—one is open-ended, the other is closed. Think about which is which, and why.

A. Were the kids okay today?

B. What did the kids do today?

You don't have to be a genius to figure out that the answer to Question A will be "Yes" or "No" or "You won't believe what they did!" You won't get a long answer no matter what.

Question B asks for a full report. As you listen, you select the areas you want to probe for more information.

This is exactly the technique good salespeople use. For example, let's say you are selling a telemarketing service. What would some of the unsatisfied needs be that you would be searching for on your sales calls?

- People want more sales for their products.

- Managers are concerned about skyrocketing costs of maintaining a field sales force.

- Sales executives want to expand or extend their markets or product lines.

- A company with a new product must saturate its market quickly.

What open-ended probes would you ask to uncover these needs?

- Tell me about your sales projections for next year.

- What concerns do you have regarding your field sales force?

- Tell me about your expansion plans.

- What are the most serious problems you face with your new product line?

Once you uncover the need, you explain how your products can satisfy it.

- Telemarketing can help you get more sales by increasing the frequency of contact with your key customers.

- Telemarketing can do the prospecting for your field sales force so they visit only well-qualified leads.

- Telemarketing can create a need for your products in territories where you can't afford to send salesmen.

- A telemarketing blitz will give you fast market penetration.

It's a simple formula: Ask the questions that uncover the needs that your product satisfies!

Once you have asked the question, remember to be silent and wait for an answer.

2. *The fine art of probing for needs.*

You must learn how and when to use both open and closed probes. The open-ended questions are ideal for fact-finding. Use them to:

- Uncover needs.

- Learn what a prospect does.

- Establish rapport.

- Control the direction of a conversation.

- Give yourself a chance to think while the prospect is talking.

Closed probes have many good uses as well. You can ask them to:

- Clarify a specific point.

- Force a decision.

- Verify information.

- Quantify a judgment.

- Prepare the prospect for an important open probe you plan to ask next.

- Set the stage for the close.

Closed probes can be dangerous for two reasons. First, a long series of closed questions will make your prospects feel like they are being cross-examined. Second, since the answers are short, you have to be ready at once with the next question or comment. After a few closed probes, you're so busy preparing for the next question that you're no longer listening. You can lose the control and direction of the conversation.

Sample forms for developing your own probes are in the Workbook.

3. *Benefits sell, features tell.*

   Train yourself to describe your product in terms of how it can help the person who buys it. For example, a telemarketing sales effort has these among its features and benefits:

Feature: Make a lot of calls in a short period of time.

Benefit: Alert all your customers to a new product, find out what they think of it, and convince 10 percent to order now.

Features are important. They tell your customers how much your product weighs, what color it is, and how it works.

Benefits are more important. They sell your customers by explaining how your products will make them more money, improve their standard of living, or give them an edge over their competition.

Which rings your bell?

Sample forms for developing your own benefit statements are in the Workbook.

4. *Your imagination can make it so!*

Some interesting research has been done in the last few years with the world's top athletes. It uncovered the practice among the best high jumpers, divers, and shot putters of visualizing exactly what they were going to do in an event before it actually took place. They developed a mental picture of themselves making a 7-foot high jump, or doing a flawless half-gainer, or tossing the 20-lb. shot to a new world record.

I have experimented with telemarketers using the technique, asking TSRs to visualize the perfect sales call.

A brisk, businesslike opening . . . a series of well-thought-out, open-ended probes uncovering the prospect's needs . . . followed by a trial close tying product benefits to needs . . . and then a few objections overcome, leading to an above-average sale.

It worked for us. Give it a try.

5. *Silence sells.*

We all want to add our two cents. And this is one of the biggest stumbling blocks to getting orders. Listening skills are most important at two points in a sales call. First, your ears must be "on their toes" when your prospects give clues to what their needs are.

The other most important instance is when your prospects TELL YOU TO CLOSE THE SALE! They often do this subtly. Sometimes they do it with a:

- Question: "When can I get one?"

- Statement agreeing with you: "You're right. That really could save me money."

- Sigh: "Ahhhh, okay."

- Description of how they would use your product: "It would fit into my plans like this . . . ."

Only by listening will you hear. Once you do hear a closing clue, go directly to your close or you will not collect $200!

We all have two ears and only one mouth!

6. *To be believable or not to be believable.*

Nothing is more precious to a salesperson than credibility. If you lose it, you lose the customer.

Professional buyers have learned to read body language to help them gauge the truthfulness of field salesmen. There is also such a thing as voice language. You must be aware of it and learn how to use it to your best advantage.

Here are some tips:

- Speak loudly and clearly. Don't whisper.

- Vary the inflection of your voice.

- Raise and lower your volume.

- Match the tempo to the subject discussed.

- Be enthusiastic, never bored.

- Never sound like you're reading a script.

- Know your product inside and out.

- Speak with authority.

- Avoid wild claims.

- Always be reasonable.

- Never lose your temper.

- Answer objections. Don't brush them aside.

- Change your wording and phrasing from call to call to stay fresh.

- Master the art of saying the same thing in many different ways.

- Teach yourself to ask your probes as a natural response to your prospect's comments.

- If fatigue creeps into your voice, rest.

- Give the impression to your prospect that you make this call only once a day to only a very select group of people.

- Always do what you say are going to do.

- Skip impossible promises.

By following these suggestions, you communicate that you're all business—someone to be taken seriously.

So when you ask for an order, they give you a serious answer. You won't be put off. Later, when you tell them you'll ship the product tomorrow, they'll start looking for it.

7. *The joke will be on you.*

   Humor is dangerous. Avoid it, particularly in the early stages of a sales relationship. All too often we end up offending someone rather than making them laugh.

There is nothing wrong with being friendly. Even a little kidding can be helpful. But never open a sales presentation with a joke.

8. *"You have a point, BUT . . . ."*

Managing objections is a skill you must master. When prospects throw an objection at you, they are simply saying, "You ain't sold me yet, but I'm listening!"

Objections are a very positive sign. Your prospect is thinking. And people who think are usually the easiest to sell, and often reliable repeat buyers. Therefore, don't be discouraged. Simply learn how to deal with the objection. Turn it around and get back on track.

Let's go back to our telemarketing sales presentation for an example.

Objection: Telemarketing costs too much.

Response: A high-cost marketing effort is one that doesn't make money. Telemarketing is measurable; you'll know exactly what it costs and exactly what it brings in. How many other kinds of advertising can you say that about? Think about testing it on a small scale and see for yourself if it doesn't pay.

Objection: We tried telemarketing once. Boy, did it bomb!

Response: There's probably a good reason for that. If you would sit down with one of our account executives, he could review what went wrong. Telemarketing isn't easy, but it can work for just about every company or product.

These are tough objections. Yet they can be handled and the conversation directed back to why the customer should consider telemarketing.

Sample forms for developing your own objections and responses are in the Workbook.

9. *You even have to be a "shrink."*

I don't recommend psychoanalysis over the phone, but you must be able to identify common personality types among the many prospects and customers you will talk to. Each should be sold differently.

TYPES OF CUSTOMERS

The Undecided Customer:

- Often insecure.

- Afraid of making a decision.

- Needs reassurance: "Just what part are you unsure about?"

- Doesn't want to make the decision alone.

- Uses phrases such as "Which, as you know—."

The Shopper—Wants to Look Around:

- Destroy his reason for not buying NOW.

"Wait Until Business Gets Better":

- Compare advantages of buying today versus waiting.

- Business doesn't get better, we *make* it better.

- Delaying purchase may mean more losses in the meantime.

- Maintain an attitude of optimism about business conditions.

- Help the customer see the bright side of things and get his mood off the negatives.

"I'm Not Really Interested":

- It could be you didn't gain his interest as yet.

"I Know It All!"

- Don't push too hard.

- Don't make your suggestions too positive.

- Guide the sales interview with questions.

- Indicate a strong interest in what he says.

- *Never* contradict him!

- Ask him about his business, his plans, ideas, and suggestions: "What do you think would be the best purchasing plan in your situation?"

- Allow him to sell himself.

- Interject a few thoughts into the conversation, he'll think they're his own.

- Concentrate on the end of the conversation, on what the product will mean to him.

- Let him be the decision maker; sample close:

   "Mr. _____, with your extensive knowledge of our services and what it will do for you, what is your decision regarding an installation date?"

"Let's Be Friends":

- Will do everything he can to avoid ordering—close, close, close.

The Antagonist:

- Obnoxious, complaining.

- Be patient; don't display discomfort; appear to like and respect him.

- Show him how your product will achieve the results he needs.

Zipper Lip:

- Open-ended questions are called for.

- Ask what's on his mind.

10. *Nothing beats a good plan.*

Telephone sales presentations have a beginning, a middle, and an end. Each section has specific objectives. Let's review a plan for a typical call.

The Beginning . . .

a. Introduce yourself.

b. Establish rapport.

c. State your business.

The Middle . . .

a. Get your prospect's attention.

b. Create awareness of the benefits of your product.

c. Probe for the prospect's needs.

d. Explain how your product satisfies those needs.

e. Manage any objections.

f. Trial close.

g. Manage additional objections.

h. Restate benefits that apply to their needs.

The End . . .

a. Ask for an order (appointment, etc., whatever the purpose of the call).

b. Repeat order for confirmation.

c. Verify shipping address and other details.

d. Thank customer.

e. Tell customer when you will be calling back.

Each stage of the call should be outlined on paper. You may not get it right the first time, so revise it as many times as you need to. But be sure to do it.

Sample forms are included in the Workbook to help you plan your calls.

11. *Open like a lamb, close like a lion!*

Closing is the most exciting and rewarding part of the sales process. Never forget, nothing happens until a sale is made. If your company can't sell its products, the show's over.

There are many different kinds of closes. You must become a master of all of them so you can slip into the right close as soon as the opportunity presents itself. Let's try a few on for size.

a.   Contained Choice: Something OR Something.

"Would you like me to ship it to you UPS or would you like to save the freight and pick it up at our warehouse?"

b.   Direct: Ask for the order!

"How many would you like?"

c.   Indirect: Make them tell you.

"There are only three days left on this special and I'd sure like to see you take advantage of these one-time prices."

"You know better than I do how much inventory you should carry this time of year."

d.   Ego Involvement: Play to their pride.

"There are some less expensive models available, but a store as nice as yours, dealing mainly with the very rich, should carry a top-drawer line, like ours."

e.   Narrative: Tell a success story.

"You probably know how hard these are to keep in stock. Every store we have dealt with in your area has sold out. I'm sure you'll have the same success."

f.   Summary: Restate customer's interest area.

"You're absolutely right. Stainless steel is the way to go in your area. Let me put you down for five with stainless steel sections."

g.   Inducement: Offer something extra for the order.

"I'll tell you what. Since this is your first order, if you buy today, I'll send you five and only bill you for four. That's a 20 percent discount. What do you say?"

NOTE: Check with your supervisor before you discount any prices.

h.   Step by Step: Ease them into an order.

"While you're thinking about it, let's wrap up some of the details. Do you want to pick them up at the warehouse or have them shipped? Should they all be red, or do you want a few green?"

i.   Continued Affirmation: "Yes" him into an order.

"Didn't you say you sold primarily to schools? And didn't you say they need a book on this subject? And didn't you say our price is 10 percent lower than our nearest competition? And that we had more colorful illustrations? Well, why don't I put you down for 10 gross of books?"

(Notice the use of closed probes in this situation.)

j.   Assumptive: Just assume you have an order.

"Yes . . . you won't have a bit of trouble selling our products. I'll just send you the starter pack tomorrow."

Since closing is so critical to success, here are a few more things to keep in mind.

a.   Review the Reference Section of the guide on listening for closing clues.

b.   Close with vitality and confidence. Never pause, stumble, or hesitate. If you're not comfortable asking for the order, role-play until you are.

c.   There are three ways to learn to close. And those are to close, close, close.

d.   Try to master one new type of close each week. Look for opportunities to use new closes.

e.   You can't take an order when you're doing all the talking. A silent phone line can sometimes close for you. The first one who speaks often loses.

f. Mix your closes with a description of the benefits that appeal most to your prospect.

g. Your close should be a logical step in your sales call plan. If it isn't, rework your plan.

h. Learn to loop back to your last point of agreement if your prospect evades your close.

i. Ask for an order on every call.

j. Don't retaliate if someone refuses to order. Leave it so you can try again at a later date. Be sure to thank them for their time.

Never become discouraged or take a rejection personally. There are legitimate reasons (sometimes) for someone not ordering. Try to discover the reason so you can overcome it next time.

12. *The trial close.*

By trial close, we simply mean an attempt to close that doesn't work. What actually happens is that the trial close usually elicits a new reason from the customer to ask again for the order. It is usually a positive reaction to something you say. So jump on it and try to close.

The prospect may resist a trial close and offer an objection. You must manage the objection and try to close again. It is very common to have two, three, or even more trial closes before a sale is made.

It is only when you try to close that you really find out what your customer is thinking. You force a decision with the close. The customer must buy or tell you why he won't. Trial closes are very valuable for this reason.

13. *It doesn't take another Shakespeare, that's for sure.*

Scripts should be written simply. They must be uncomplicated. The best ones are used only as guidelines for the experienced telephone sales communicator. When preparing a script, follow the guidelines presented in Section V, "Special Selling Skills."

Telemarketing scripting skill and creativity are crucial in two areas. The first is in how you go about getting your prospect's attention. Here you need a statement that is both startling and yet 100 percent credible. Most often the appeal is made to your prospect's best self-interest.

"Give me a few minutes and I'll tell you how you can increase your sales by 20 percent while reducing your cost per sale!"

The second area in which to apply your best thinking is the close, particularly the offer you make. What can you offer that prospects can't refuse, yet will make you a dandy profit?

"Place your order now and you'll get a 20 percent discount good through the entire year."

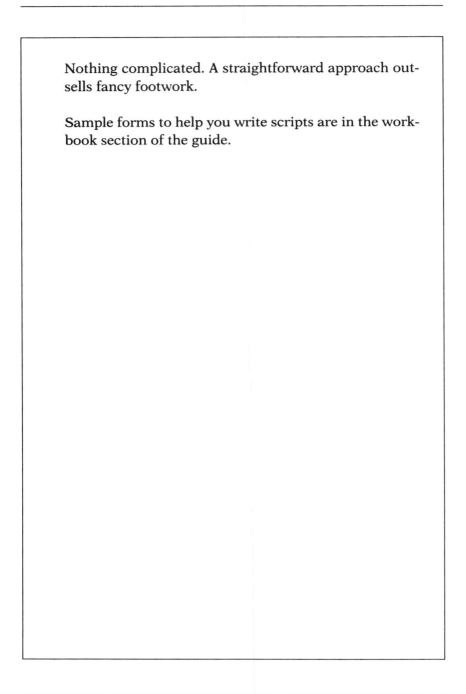

Nothing complicated. A straightforward approach out-sells fancy footwork.

Sample forms to help you write scripts are in the workbook section of the guide.

VI.   Words Are Your Tools

Words have personalities of their own. Some words are naturally positive (party, fun, play, love); others we shy away from (death, torture, dismemberment, execute).

Since words are your basic tool, you must become sensitive to the words you use. You always want to use words that will help you achieve your goals. Even more so, you want to stay away from those that will slow your progress.

1. The words and phrases below are most commonly associated with probes:

Open Probes:	*Closed Probes:*
Tell me more about . . .	How many?
Why?	Exactly when . . .
How does . . .	Where?
Where?	Are you . . .
What would you do . . .	Do you still . . .
Explain to me . . .	Are you aware . . .
What will . . .	Have you heard about . . .
Can you illustrate . . .	Who does?
Any examples . . .	What color?
	Name one.

Open probes encourage long, essay-type answers.

Closed probes are more like multiple-choice questions—a, b, c.

Probes have different uses, as we learned earlier, and our choice of words controls how our questions are answered.

2. Eliminate "know-it-all"-type words and phrases from your vocabulary. Here are a few examples:

You know what I mean.

Understand?

Get the point?

Here's how it is.

Just ask me.

If you listen to me.

Who told you that!

3. Replace these with words and phrases that lead your prospects to where you want them to go—the order desk.

Phrases:

Thanks for the help.

Your sure know your business.

Congratulations on selecting our product.

If you need any more help, call me.

It's a pleasure working with you.

You deserve the credit for . . .

You spotted the savings right off.

Words:

ambition	new
benefit	opportunity
compel	pleasure
discover	progressive
discovery	proven
energy	results
excite	save
future	solution
guarantee	stimulating
impact	suggestion
implement	technology
innovative	thrust
money	

4. Here are some progressive words. Use as many as you can to describe your product or service.

admired	hospitality	sympathy
affectionate	hunting	tasteful
ambition	independent	tested
amusement	love	thinking
appetizing	low-cut	time-saving
bargain	modern	up-to-date
beauty	necessary	value
clean	personality	youth
courtesy	popular	
durable	progressive	
economical	qualify	
efficient	recommended	
elegance	relief	
enormous	reputation	
excel	royalty	
expressive	safe	
fun	scientific	
genuine	sociable	
growth	status	
guaranteed	stimulating	
health	stylish	
home	successful	

5. Forget you ever heard or saw these counterproductive words.

abandoned	decline	ignorant
abuse	desert	illiterate
affected	disaster	imitation
alibi	discredit	immature
allege	dispute	implicate
apology	evict	impossible
bankrupt	exaggerate	improvident
beware	extravagant	insolvent
biased	fail	in vain
blame	failure	liable
calamity	fault	long-winded
careless	fear	meager
cheap	flagrant	mediocre
collapse	flat	misfortune
collusion	flimsy	muddle
commonplace	fraud	neglect
complaint	gloss over	negligence
crisis	gratuitous	obstinate
crooked	hardship	odds and ends
cut-and-dried	harp upon	opinionated
deadlock	hazy	oversight

plausible	slack	timid
precipitate	smattering	tolerable
prejudiced	split hairs	unfair
premature	squander	unfortunate
pretentious	stagnant	unsuccessful
retrench	standstill	untimely
rude	struggling	verbiage
ruin	stunted	waste
shirk	superficial	weak
shrink	tamper	worry
sketchy	tardy	wrong

6. Memorize this group. They'll help you increase your sales.

ability	approval	commendation
abundant	aspire	comprehensive
achieve	attainment	concentration
active	authoritative	confidence
admirable	benefit	conscientious
advance	capable	cooperation
advantage	cheer	courtesy
ambition	comfort	definite
appreciate	commendable	dependable

deserving	grateful	majority
desirable	guarantee	merit
determined	handsome	meritorious
distinction	harmonious	notable
diversity	helpful	opportunity
ease	honesty	perfection
economy	honor	permanent
effective	humor	perseverance
efficient	imagination	pleasant
energy	improvement	please
enhance	industry	popularity
enthusiasm	ingenuity	practical
equality	initiative	praiseworthy
excellence	integrity	prestige
exceptional	intelligence	proficient
exclusive	judgment	progress
expedite	justice	prominent
faith	kind	punctual
fidelity	lasting	reasonable
fitting	liberal	recognition
genuine	life	recommend
good	loyalty	reliable

reputable	success	unstinted
responsible	superior	useful
satisfactory	supremacy	utility
service	through	vigor
simplicity	thought	vital
sincerity	thoughtful	vivid
stability	thrift	wisdom
substantial	truth	

7. Another speech pattern to avoid is using the same word(s) over and over and over again in the same conversation.

You know . . .

You know . . .

You know . . .

Or,

Uh-huh.

Uh-huh.

Uh-huh.

This repetition drives most people up the wall!

VII. You're Not on a Debating Team!

The fastest way to lose a sale is to get into an argument with a prospect or customer. You must avoid debating, or "we" versus "they" confrontations.

This occurs most often when you're fielding objections. You can skip over this trap by always starting your response to an objection by confirming that the objection is legitimate. Here's an example:

Objection: "I need to see my customers face-to-face."

Response: "You're absolutely right. Nothing is more valuable than personal contact with customers. Even so, many firms have learned to use telemarketing to supplement personal sales calls. As a result, not as many personal sales calls have to be made each year. Sales costs drop substantially."

Nobody wants to have anybody argue with them or call them stupid (directly or indirectly). There's no place in a professional telephone sales call for this kind of behavior.

VIII. Call Patterns

Typical Call Pattern for Repeat Customer Business

Initial Call:
1. Establish rapport.
2. Learn about customer's needs and usage patterns for your product.
3. Explain product.
4. Set up regular calling schedule.
5. Close.

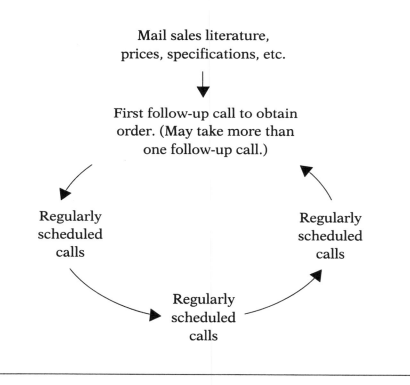

Mail sales literature,
prices, specifications, etc.

First follow-up call to obtain
order. (May take more than
one follow-up call.)

Regularly
scheduled
calls

Regularly
scheduled
calls

Regularly
scheduled
calls

Typical Call Pattern for a One-Time Sale

Sales Call:
1. Introduce and establish rapport.
2. Create interest.
3. Find needs.
4. Satisfy needs.
5. Overcome objections.
6. Close.
7. Verify information.

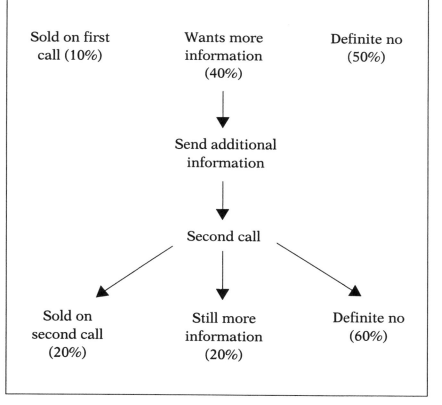

| Sold on first call (10%) | Wants more information (40%) | Definite no (50%) |

Send additional information

Second call

| Sold on second call (20%) | Still more information (20%) | Definite no (60%) |

Full Account Management Entails:

1. Selling, calling for reorders, and selling additional products to established accounts.

2. Solving any problems, invoicing, product quality, delivery, returns, etc.

3. Tracking customer inventory.

4. Introducing customer to new products.

5. Call schedule coincides with customer's usage pattern.

6. Collection on overdue account.

THE
REFERENCE
WORKBOOK
SECTION

I. How to Use the Workbook

The purpose of the workbook is to give you outlines to follow as you personalize the general information contained in the Reference Guide.

You may want to photocopy the workbook pages as you prepare rough drafts of your own scripts, objections/responses, and probes. If there is more than one of you, create your material as a group with your supervisor as the group leader.

Also, when preparing the final drafts that will be put into your personal workbook, consider using a heavier cardboard stock of paper and an oversize type face. This will increase the readability, especially during the "heat" of a good sales call, and prevent the sheet from tearing out of the binder.

II. Company Information Work Page

Brief history of your company

_____

_____

_____

_____

How owned? Private or public?

Owner: _____

How long in business? _____

How many employees?_____

List of product services:

_____

_____

_____

_____

List of prominent customers:

_____

_____

_____

_____

_____

What single fact would management like to communicate to every prospect or customer about your company?

_____

_____

_____

_____

III. Customer Needs Work Pages

Study your product or service from your customers' point of view. Which of their needs does the product satisfy?

Will it save them money?

Will it make them money?

Will it speed up their manufacturing process?

Will it increase their sales?

Will it improve their personal careers, knowledge or status?

Will it help them to be the hit of the party, company, etc.?

Will it prevent them from making costly errors?

Will it reduce taxes on sales costs?

As you define your customer's needs, work hard to be specific. It's more effective to cut sales costs by 19 percent than to just cut sales costs. The more specific you are, the more credibility you earn.

Here are a few areas to consider. Write your customer needs on the lines in the areas that pertain to your product or service.

Financial Needs (money, cost reduction, etc.):

_____

_____

_____

Production Needs (increase productivity, reduce down-time, etc.):

_____

_____

_____

Management Needs (increase efficiency, reduce labor, etc.):

_____

_____

_____

Marketing Needs (increase sales, reduce sales costs, etc.):

_____

_____

_____

Personal Needs (improve career, earnings, etc.):

_____

_____

_____

Other Personal Needs (spiritual, belonging, self-esteem, etc.):

_____

_____

_____

IV. Probing Work Pages

What questions can you ask your customers/prospects to get them talking in general and talking about their needs in particular? Try to slant the question to uncover the needs that your product/service satisfies.

For example, on the Needs Page you wrote that your product reduces production costs, prepare some probes like "What area of your manufacturing process would you like to improve?" or "Tell me about the trend of your production costs."

Most companies have active customers, prospects, and inactive customers. You should tailor a set of probes for each one of these groups plus any others you'll be calling regularly.

Active Customers—Open Probes:

How is your product/service working for you?

What questions can I answer for you?

How do you use our_____?

I'd like to learn more about your business.
Could you tell me_____?

_____

_____

_____

_____

_____

_____

_____

_____

_____

_____

_____

_____

_____

_____

_____

_____

_____

_____

_____

_____

_____

_____

Active Customers—Closed Probes:

When will you be needing more_____?

Are you familiar with our new_____?

Do you still buy_____?

How many _____ can I put you down for?

_____

_____

_____

_____

_____

_____

_____

_____

_____

_____

_____

_____

_____

_____

_____

_____

_____

_____

_____

_____

_____

_____

_____

Inactive Customers—Open Probes:

Why did you stop using our product?

Tell me how you used to use_____.

What can we do to get you back as a customer?

What problems are you having with our competitor, ABC Company?

How is it working out with ABC Company?

How does ABC's product work?

Tell me a little about their pricing/delivery/inventory policy.

_____
_____
_____
_____
_____
_____
_____
_____
_____
_____
_____
_____
_____
_____
_____
_____
_____

Inactive Customers—Closed Probes:

How long has it been since you bought_____?

What are you using now in place of_____?

Do you know about the improvements we made to_____?

Has anybody told you about our new inventory and pricing policy?

When can we expect an order from you? (A good question to uncover objections and the customer's real feelings about your company.)

_____
_____
_____
_____
_____
_____
_____
_____
_____
_____
_____
_____
_____
_____
_____
_____
_____
_____

Prospects—Open Probes:

Tell me about your company.

What do you manufacture/service?

Who are your customers?

How do you manufacture_____?

How large is your company?

How large a geographic territory do you cover?

What areas would you like to see improvement in?

What are you using now to_____(whatever the company does)?

What do we have to do to get your business?

What are some problems you're facing with your products?

_____
_____
_____
_____
_____
_____
_____
_____
_____
_____

Prospects—Closed Probes:

Have you heard about our product?

How much do you pay for that product now?

What are ABC Company's delivery schedules (or prices, returns, etc.)?

How many_____do you have in inventory?

How many do you normally buy at a time?

When do you do your buying?

Who does the buying?

_____
_____
_____
_____
_____
_____
_____
_____
_____
_____
_____
_____
_____
_____
_____
_____

V. Benefits and Features Work Pages

Most companies sell the features instead of the benefits that their products deliver to the customer. The odd thing is that most buyers are interested in benefits, not features. Be different. Sell benefits and become successful. Again, your benefits must reflect your customer's needs.

Examples

Product: automobile

Feature: convertible

    Benefit: People will notice you.

    Benefit: You'll look and feel younger.

Feature: 350 cc engine

    Benefit: The performance makes driving a pleasure.

    Benefit: You can get on and off interstate highways safely.

Your Product

Feature: _____

_____

Benefit _____

_____

Benefit _____

_____

Feature: _____

_____

Benefit _____

_____

Benefit _____

_____

Feature: _____

_____

Benefit _____

_____

Benefit _____

_____

Your Product

Feature: _____
_____

Benefit _____
_____

Benefit _____
_____

Feature: _____
_____

Benefit _____
_____

Benefit _____
_____

Feature: _____
_____

Benefit _____
_____

Benefit _____
_____

Your Product

Feature: _____

_____

Benefit _____

_____

Benefit _____

_____

Feature: _____

_____

Benefit _____

_____

Benefit _____

_____

Feature: _____

_____

Benefit _____

_____

Benefit _____

_____

Your Product

Feature: _____
_____

Benefit _____
_____

Benefit _____
_____

Feature: _____
_____

Benefit _____
_____

Benefit _____
_____

Feature: _____
_____

Benefit _____
_____

Benefit _____
_____

Your Product

Feature: _____

_____

Benefit _____

_____

Benefit _____

_____

Feature: _____

_____

Benefit _____

_____

Benefit _____

_____

Feature: _____

_____

Benefit _____

_____

Benefit _____

_____

Your Product

Feature: _____

_____

Benefit _____

_____

Benefit _____

_____

Feature: _____

_____

Benefit _____

_____

Benefit _____

_____

Feature: _____

_____

Benefit _____

_____

Benefit _____

_____

VI. Objections and Responses Work Pages

Every product, service, or industry has certain objections that are peculiar to each. We can't cover them all here.

You'll have to sit down with your marketing team to list the objections and responses that are unique to your business. As you do your telemarketing, take notes on objections you have trouble handling. Develop responses to them at your regular sales meetings. Share this information freely.

To get you started, the following is a list of objections that seem generic to just about every product or company.

Objections and Responses

"It costs too much."

Everything seems to cost too much these days. I'll agree with you there, but let's look at it from a total value standpoint. Our product/service is of more value for these reasons . . . .

"The person who does the buying is not in."

When will he/she be in?

What is his/her name?

When would be a good time to call back?

"Business couldn't be worse."

I'm sorry to hear that, but this is the right time to talk about_____because it can increase your sales while decreasing your costs.

"I'm in a meeting; I can't talk now."

I understand. When may I call back?

"I'm afraid I'm just not interested."

I can relate to that. And you shouldn't be until you've had a chance to see how _____ can substantially improve your business.

"I'll call you when we need some."

That's great. When can I expect a call?

Would you prefer I call in two weeks?

"We have all the inventory we can handle."

How much do you have?

How long will that last you?

Great, I'll call back then.

"Not now. Let me think it over."

That's a good way of doing business. While I'm right here on the phone, are there any additional questions I can answer for you? When would be the best time to call back for your answer?

"I have to discuss it with my boss/partner/owner."

I'm only a phone call away if you have any further questions. Don't hesitate to call. I'll call you back on _____at _____for your answer.

"I don't think we're ready to switch suppliers right now."

We're anxious to do business with you. Our product outperforms what you're presently using and our price is competitive. What would it take to get you to make the switch?

"We're buying from one of your competitors."

We have several very good competitors. Which one are you buying from? How does our price compare to theirs? (Or service, delivery, etc.)

"My buddy sells the stuff. We always buy from him."

It's wise to trade with people you know. But you must also consider your obligation to your company to get the best value available. Let me compare the advantages of _____ to what you're currently using.

"My present source has performed well. There's no need to change."

Needless change doesn't do anyone any good. But what if I could show you how you could save_____ percent on each shipment? That would be a meaningful change. Would that make a difference?

"Sounds good, but let me check a couple of other sources."

Is anything bothering you about my bid? When do you plan on checking? Fine. I'll call you back on_____ at_____.

"I can't buy everything from everybody."

Certainly not. You must do what is best for your company. And when you compare all the facts, our products come way out on top!

"Your salesperson stinks!"

I'm sorry to hear you have a personality conflict with him/her. If you'd like, you can deal directly with me from now on.

"Your service has been miserable lately."

Just give me a call directly. I'll take care of you.

Use this area to write objections and responses specific to your product/service.

Objection   _____

_____

_____

Response   _____

_____

_____

Objection   _____

_____

_____

Response   _____

_____

_____

Objection _____
_____
_____

Response _____
_____
_____

Objection _____
_____
_____

Response _____
_____
_____

Objection _____
_____
_____

Response _____
_____
_____

Objection _____
_____
_____

Response _____
_____
_____

297

Objection _____

_____

_____

Response _____

_____

_____

Objection _____

_____

_____

Response _____

_____

_____

VII. Closing Work Pages

Below are 10 proven closes. Under each one is a space for you to write your own or modify the ones provided to fit your product or service.

1. Contained Choice—Something or something.

   "Would today or next Tuesday be more convenient?"

   _____
   _____
   _____
   _____
   _____

2. Direct—Ask for the order.

   "How many do you want?"

   _____
   _____
   _____
   _____
   _____

3. Indirect—Make them tell you.

   "What do you think?"

   _____
   _____
   _____
   _____
   _____

4. Ego Involvement—Play to their pride.

"Someone like you who can really spot a bargain will want a dozen."

_____
_____
_____
_____
_____
_____

5. Narrative—Tell a success story.

"All our other dealers have sold out in a week or less. You will too. I'll put you down for 10 gross."

_____
_____
_____
_____
_____
_____

6. Summary—Restate customer's interest area.

"You sure know your business. You're right when you say you need 10 per week for the next 10 weeks."

_____
_____
_____
_____
_____

7. Inducement—Offer something extra.

   "Order today and we'll ship freight-free!"

   _____
   _____
   _____
   _____

8. Step by Step—Ease them into an order.

   "Red makes the most sense, as you said. And two dozen is a good first order. We can ship tomorrow and you'll have them by Wednesday. How will that be?"

   _____
   _____
   _____
   _____

9. Continued Affirmation—"Yes" them into an order.

   "Didn't you say our price was lower?"

   "And didn't you say our quality was better?"

   "And didn't you say you were out of stock?"

   "Well, how about ordering now?"

   _____
   _____
   _____
   _____

10. Assumptive—Just assume you have an order.

"Yes. You need 1,000 to begin with. Let's see how long they last before we set a reorder schedule."

_____

_____

_____

_____

_____

VIII. Competition Work Pages

Who's your competition?

1. Name
   _____

   Location
   _____
   _____
   _____

   Product(s)
   _____
   _____

   Advantages
   _____
   _____
   _____

   Disadvantages
   _____
   _____
   _____

   Your Competitive Edge
   _____
   _____
   _____
   _____
   _____

2. Name

_____

Location

_____

_____

_____

Product(s)

_____

_____

Advantages

_____

_____

_____

Disadvantages

_____

_____

_____

Your Competitive Edge

_____

_____

_____

_____

_____

_____

_____

3. Name

_____

Location

_____
_____
_____

Product(s)

_____
_____

Advantages

_____
_____
_____

Disadvantages

_____
_____
_____

Your Competitive Edge

_____
_____
_____
_____
_____
_____
_____

4. Name
_____

Location
_____
_____
_____

Product(s)
_____
_____

Advantages
_____
_____
_____

Disadvantages
_____
_____
_____

Your Competitive Edge
_____
_____
_____
_____
_____
_____
_____

5. Name

  Location

  Product(s)

  Advantages

  Disadvantages

  Your Competitive Edge

6. Name

_____

Location

_____

_____

_____

Product(s)

_____

_____

Advantages

_____

_____

_____

Disadvantages

_____

_____

_____

Your Competitive Edge

_____

_____

_____

_____

_____

_____

_____

_____

7. Name

   _____

   Location

   _____
   _____
   _____

   Product(s)

   _____
   _____

   Advantages

   _____
   _____
   _____

   Disadvantages

   _____
   _____
   _____

   Your Competitive Edge

   _____
   _____
   _____
   _____
   _____
   _____
   _____

8. Name

_____

Location

_____

_____

_____

Product(s)

_____

_____

Advantages

_____

_____

_____

Disadvantages

_____

_____

_____

Your Competitive Edge

_____

_____

_____

_____

_____

_____

_____

_____

9. Name

_____

Location

_____

_____

_____

Product(s)

_____

_____

Advantages

_____

_____

_____

Disadvantages

_____

_____

_____

Your Competitive Edge

_____

_____

_____

_____

_____

_____

_____

10. Name

_____

Location

_____

_____

_____

Product(s)

_____

_____

Advantages

_____

_____

_____

Disadvantages

_____

_____

_____

Your Competitive Edge

_____

_____

_____

_____

_____

_____

_____

_____

IX. Scripting Work Pages

Basic Script—Active Customer

Introduction:

This is _____ with _____.

May I speak with _____?

If No: When would be a good time to call back?

If Yes: Reintroduce yourself.

Establish rapport, give reason for call, and create interest:

(Ask simple personal questions based on previous calls, if you can.)

How are things going today?_____

The reason for my call is _____.

There's a special 20 percent discount on _____ this month.

Fact-find and search for needs by probing:

Do you use _____?

How many do you use at a time?

Sales message about benefits:

> You'll want to try our_____because they can cut your production time by_____ percent!

Manage objections:

> You're right about storing so many of them at a time, but we can drop-ship them to you as you need them.

Close:

> We'll ship the first 1,000 tomorrow and drop ship the rest as per your release.

Verify information:

> Let me check the shipping address.

Show appreciation, reinforce buying decision and set up next call:

> Thank you very much for the order. You'll find this first shipment substantially reduces your production time. I'll call you back next week to see how everything worked out.

> (On next week's call, you would ask for the release of the next 1,000 units.)

Basic Script—Inactive Customer

Introduction:

This is _____ with_____.

May I speak with_____?

If No or you don't know who to talk to: When would the best time be for me to call back?

Or:

Is _____ still the person who buys _____? Find out who the person is you need to talk to and ask to be connected to him or her.

If Yes: Reintroduce yourself.

Establish a rapport, give reason for call, and create interest:

The reason for my call is to let you know about the changes we made in our freight policy. Did you know you could get_____ delivered freight free? That prices it way below our competition.

Fact-find and search for needs by probing:

You used to use _____, didn't you?
Why did you stop?

What are you using now?

How's that going?

Sales message about benefits:

Besides saving you freight, _____ has been improved so it can increase your productivity by _____ percent, as well.

Is that enough to get you to switch back? (If not, what will it take?)

Manage objections:

You're right, we used to have a real delivery problem. But now we stockpile a six-month supply. You can expect delivery within 24 hours on truckload lots.

Close:

How about an order today?

Verify information:

You'll be wanting the medium size and one truckload to start with, is that correct?

Show appreciation, reinforce buying decision, and set up next call:

> Thanks for the order. You'll be happy with _____. I'll call back in two days to see how it's going.

Basic Script—Prospect

Introduction:

This is _____ with _____.

Who is in charge of _____ (marketing, engineering, purchasing, buying steel, whatever)?

May I speak with_____?

If No: When should I call back?

If Yes: Reintroduce yourself.

Establish rapport, give reason for call, and create interest:

I'm calling to let you know about a new service that's now available in _____ (city). It's the first time anybody ever offered _____ here!

Fact-find and search for needs by probing:

Have you ever had access to _____?

Do you know how much money _____ can save you?

How has _____ (city) ever gotten by without a _____?

Sales message using benefits:

> _____ is just about the most fun a family can have for only $12.95 a month. It gives your family . . . .

Manage objections:

> That's the way the old-fashioned ones worked. But not anymore. You don't have to buy anything extra now. Just plug it in and your family is in for a fun evening.

Close:

> If you order now, I can also send you five free cartridges. So, how about it.
>
> Should I take your order now?

Verify information:

> Your address is still _____?
>
> Mastercard #_____? Expiration date?
>
> It will be shipped tomorrow.

Show appreciation, reinforce buying decision, and set up next call, if there is one:

> Great! You and your family will love _____ for years and years. Don't forget the five-year warranty.

Script Work Page

Type of customer: _____

Introduction: _____

_____

_____

    If No: _____

    If Yes: _____

Establish rapport, give reason for call and create interest:

    The reason for my call is _____

_____

Fact-find, search for needs by probing:

    (Put your pages of probes opposite the script once
it is finalized.)

_____

_____

Sales message about benefits:

    (List five most important benefits from benefit work page.)

    1. _____

    2. _____

    3. _____

4. _____

5. _____

Manage objections:

(Objections/response work pages should be put where they are easily and quickly accessible during calls.)

Verify information:

(List information you need checked on each call, such as name, address, credit card number, etc.)

1. _____

2. _____

3. _____

4. _____

5. _____

Show appreciation, reinforce buying decision, and set up next call, if necessary.

Thank you very much for

_____
_____
_____
_____

TELEMARKETING NOTES

_____
_____
_____
_____
_____
_____
_____
_____
_____
_____
_____
_____
_____
_____
_____
_____
_____
_____
_____
_____
_____
_____
_____
_____
_____
_____
_____
_____
_____
_____

TELEMARKETING NOTES

X. Pre-Call Planning Work Pages

Complete one of these prior to making a *new* type of a call to a *new* market on a *new* or *different* type of customer. Make sure everyone knows in advance why they are making the call.

The purpose of these calls is...

[ ] To sell _____

　　　The offer is _____

[ ] To get leads for our field sales force. Here's how the prospects should be qualified:

　　　1. _____

　　　2. _____

　　　3. _____

[ ] To do market research. Let's review the "Survey."

[ ] Other: _____
_____

　　　We must accomplish _____
_____

[ ] Here's a list of special information you need in front of you:

1. _____

2. _____

3. _____

[ ] The estimated guidelines for this job are:

_____ dialings per hour

_____ successful calls per day/week

Campaign starts on _____ and should be completed by _____.

Best time of day/evening to call is _____.

Best days to call are _____.

Don't call _____ _____

XI. Organizing Your Reference Guide

By now, you have all the information and material to assemble a professional Reference Guide for your own company. All you need to do now is organize the material. I recommend the following order.

1. Move all the seldom-used material either to the rear or to the front of the guide, out of the way.

2. Your personalized scripts should be positioned on the left side of a page and the corresponding probing questions on the right.

3. The guide should be kept in front of you on a TeleEasel or other type of easel, so your hands are free to take notes and complete order forms, surveys, or call reports.

4. Immediately behind the scripts should be the Objection/Response section.

5. It's important to track your progress, sales, number of calls completed per day, and quality of names and numbers on the list. Talk to your supervisor about setting up a system.

XII. Daily Questions to Ask Yourself

DON'T TOUCH THE PHONE UNTIL YOU CAN ANSWER YES TO EACH OF THESE QUESTIONS!

Do you know who you are calling?

Do you know why?

Do you know how you are going to create interest about your product?

Have you memorized five open-ended probes to use?

Do you know exactly what your offer is?

Do you know how to overcome or manage the 10 most common objections without looking them up?

Do you have a list of phone numbers to call?

Do you know enough about your company to sound like a longtime employee?

Checklist of Things to Do to Set Up a Telemarketing Center

A. Audit and evaluate existing in-house capabilities.

1. Personnel:
Interview the employees or applicants selected as telemarketing manager and TSRs and prepare written evaluations.

2. Customer/prospect lists:
Evaluate the telemarketing readiness of in-house lists. Research other lists available, if applicable.

3. Selling procedures:
Review the current sales program. Evaluate it in light of a telemarketing sales effort. Record possible changes.

4. Advertising:
Study existing advertising programs and campaigns from the perspective of integrating them with telemarketing.

5. Internal systems:
Review current order processing, billing, warehousing, delivery, and service procedures, etc., as they relate to telemarketing.

6. Equipment and space allocation:
Look these over and determine what changes must be made.

7. Management:
Stress the need for top-down support. Make managers aware of the pros and cons of telemarketing. Offer case histories. Conduct mini-seminars and training sessions if necessary.

8. Outside Support:
Determine if you'll need to tap outside sources for telemarketing managers, marketing managers, telemarketers, professional advice, training, etc.

9. Prepare a written report summarizing findings and recommendations.

B. Conduct a pilot project.

Set up a three- to six-month test telemarketing project at a professional telemarketing agency to thoroughly test the telemarketing system, debug it, and refine it before bringing it in-house.

C. Prepare an action plan.

Once the results of the pilot project are examined and a direction agreed upon, prepare an action plan. Some of its components would be:

1. Develop a reference guide.
This is a compilation of all the background information TSRs will need in front of them when they are making calls. It includes scripts, common objections with appropriate responses, product facts and specifications, notes on competitors, company policies, lists of benefits, and reasons why customers would want to buy the products.

2. Outline the training required.
This includes both product knowledge and telemarketing skills.

3. Develop a tracking system.
The telemarketing effort must be closely monitored. Since profitability and performance standards are vital to the center's success, special forms should be prepared (e.g., TSR Daily Activity Logs).

4. Train management.
Close supervision and support by responsible management can make or break any telemarketing effort. Supervisors need to be taught how to evaluate and motivate telemarketers and to maximize efficiency and prevent burnout.

5. Document the telemarketing system.
Job descriptions, performance standards, work rules, and other procedures are important for proper control. These should be prepared in written format.

6. Develop collateral materials.

Include specific recommendations regarding any additional brochures, direct-mail pieces, or introductory or follow-up letters that will be needed.

7. Assess equipment and work area.

Questions concerning telephone equipment, telephone lines, furniture, or remodeling should be considered.

8. Calculate a budget.

A detailed first-year budget, by month, must be prepared.

9. Develop a timetable.

A calendar of the key events in the establishment of the center should be attached to the budget.

10. Miscellaneous.

Any other changes that should be considered.
Implement the action plan.

A "Do NOT Call Me" Sample Policy

I. Background

The Telephone Consumer Protection Act (TCPA) went into effect on December 20, 1992. It instructs the Federal Communications Commission (FCC) to develop regulations to protect the privacy rights of residential telephone subscribers and to provide them a way of stopping unwanted calls. The FCC defines telephone sales as the "initiation of a telephone call or message for the purposes of encouraging the purchase or rental of, or investment in, property, goods or services, as is transmitted to any person." Each organization is required to prepare a written policy and train employees regarding the law and the policy.

II. FCC Regulations

- Telephone solicitation calls may not be made to residences before 8:00 a.m. or after 9:00 p.m., based on local time of the recipient.

- Companies making calls must maintain a list of people who do not wish to be called at all. This list must include their telephone number.

- TSRs are obligated to identify to the consumer the name of the company they are working for and to give them a phone number at which the company can be reached.

- The name of any person requesting to be removed from a list must be distributed among all calling facilities.

- A company is considered to be in compliance with the TCPA as long as someone requesting to be removed from its list is not called again.

- TCPA gives the consumer the right to bring suit against a violating company in his state's courts for up to $500 or actual monetary damages, whichever is greater. The consumer can also ask the FCC to pursue violators and the state's attorney general can take action.

- Unsolicited fax solicitations are also excluded by TCPA.

III. Company Procedure

Requests not to be called will be handled in the following manner:

- If someone you call requests that he/she not ever be called again by us, give that person's name, address, and phone number to the Marketing Department. Be sure to clarify that this person is not telling you he/she does not wish to talk now, but wants to be completely removed from our lists.

- When, or if, this occurs, tell that person we will be happy to permanently remove him/her from our list.

- The Marketing Department will see to it that our databases are updated to reflect this person's preference not to be called and will distribute the name to our various offices.

- The Marketing Department will supply each TSR with a list of people who wish not to be called. Check this list before beginning a calling session.

- The transmission of unsolicited fax solicitation is also prohibited.

- The use of autodialers that deliver a prerecorded message is also prohibited.

Dealing with Credit Card Fraud

Telemarketing faces a special problem with credit card fraud. The U.S. Office of Consumer Affairs estimates that credit card fraud will reach $1 billion. Although this may be less of a concern in business-to-business selling, it is one that should concern us all.

If your telemarketing center accepts credit cards, be on guard for fraud. Research the problem and prepare a plan of action to deal with it. Here are a few ideas to consider:

A. Keep your staff alerted to the potential of fraud. Explain the seriousness of the problem and develop strategies to combat it.

B. Ask customers who pay by credit card for the following information:

1. Home and business phone numbers. If fraud is suspected, these can be checked to see if names, phone numbers, and addresses match.

2. Name of the bank that issued the credit card and the Business Identification Number (BIN) that is stamped on the card. Get a directory of Visa and MasterCard issuing banks and check to see that the BIN and the bank match. (Many companies program their computers to make these verifications.)

C. Train your TSRs to detect bad numbers and to stop those orders before they are processed and filled.

D. Screen your own staff for honesty before hiring. It goes without saying that job candidates with spotty or unverifiable work histories should be avoided.

E. Develop and distribute to TSRs a data file of names and addresses of persons or businesses you do not want to sell to because of prior credit problems.

F. Develop a fair and reasonable return policy on telemarketing orders. Make sure it is clearly stated in all ads, catalogs, and brochures. Do not accept unauthorized returns.

G. Try to involve your bank by requesting detailed records from the bank on all credit card chargebacks. These are but a few of the things that can be done to protect against credit card fraud. Sources for more information are provided in Appendix 1. If you allow customers to pay by credit card, do not overlook this problem in your haste to accept orders.

Glossary of Telemarketing and Telecommunications Terms

Account Code(s)   Numeric codes used to track the activity of TSRs, departments, projects, or campaigns.

ASCII   American Standard Code of Information Interchange; a commonly used computer code to transmit information electronically.

Auto (automatic) Answering Devices   Telcom equipment that answers voice or data calls without human intervention.

Automatic Computer Record Dialing Machine   A machine that dials programmed telephone numbers and plays a recorded message.

Auto (automatic) Dialing Devices   Telcom equipment that dials a complete phone number using only one or two keystrokes. Sometimes referred to as speed dialers.

Automatic Line Selection   A function of telephone systems in which the system directly selects the best route for calls. Sometimes referred to as least-cost routing.

ANI   Automatic Number Identification software that detects the telephone number of inbound calls.

ARS   Automatic Route Selection is a switch that chooses the least costly path from available circuits.

Barge-Out Device   A machine that announces the same message to all callers.

Basic Rate Interface (BRI)   An ISDN (Integrated Services Digital Network) classification that has two "B" or bearer channels and one "D" channel. It carries control information and interfaces with the network. Used by individual and local CENTREX users.

Behavior Modeling   A training technique that ignores attitudes and shows TSRs how to develop desirable skills in typical sales situations.

BOC   Bell Operating Companies are the seven regional phone companies that were once part of AT&T. Now they are independent and known as the Seven Sisters.

Blocked Calls   Calls that receive a busy signal or cannot connect for some reason.

Boiler Room   Call centers characterized by lack of professionalism, controls, ethics, positive atmosphere, and equipment.

Boom   A semi-rigid, tubed apparatus that extends from the headset to in front of the TSRs mouth. It contains the microphone.

Burnout   A condition of exhaustion, frustration, and lost motivation that TSRs occasionally experience. Often related to high percentage of rejection during intense sales campaigns, particularly when a lot of cold-calling is being done.

Call Diversion   Transfers calls from one telephone number to another. This could be prearranged or to manage an emergency situation.

Call Forcing   Moves a call automatically onto the line of the next available TSR, who gets an audible tone.

Call Restrictions   Denies access of extensions to certain services, such as preventing 900 calls from a company's phones.

Call Sequencer   Distributes incoming calls in desired fashion.

Centrex   Local telephone company allows companies to use its switching equipment, rather than having the switches in the companies' offices.

Closed-Ended Probes   Questions requiring a yes- or no-type answer. Used to obtain specific information.

Clustering   Sorting names on a master list by geographic, demographic, and psychographic characteristics to improve response.

Cold Calling   Calls made to a list of people who have not shown or indicated any interest in the product or service being promoted.

Consultative Selling   The sales approach in which TSRs uncover prospects needs and match the benefits of the product being sold to those needs.

Customer Cycling   Organized or planned attempts to resell or contact customers on a regular basis.

Database   A collection of all the information available on each customer. It is used to provide the best service possible.

Data Communications Equipment (DCE)   modems and such equipment that facilitates transmission of data electronically.

Data Over Voice (DOV)   Voice and data transmitted over the same line.

Demographics   A statistical description of customers or prospects.

Display Phone   A telephone with a visual display.

Divestiture   The famous ruling by U.S. District Judge Harold Green, as part of the AT&T antitrust settlement, whereby AT&T was ordered to sever all ties with the seven Bell Operating Companies (BOC).

Direct Inward Dialing   Allows inbound calls to be routed to a specific extension, bypassing the system operating station (PBX or console).

Do Not Disturb   A feature available on some phone systems that prevents interruptions of calls by paging or intercom.

Dual-Tone Multifrequency Phones   Touch-tone phones.

800 Service   Inbound long-distance service in which the company receiving the call pays the toll. Also called toll-free calling.

Electronic Mail   The process of sending and receiving messages from one computer terminal to another.

Equal Access   Gives customers access to all long-distance carriers.

Ergonomics   The study of adjusting working conditions and equipment to physical characteristics of workers.

Facsimile (fax)   Electronically transmits hard (paper) copy over telephone lines.

FCC (Federal Communications Commission)   The federal agency that oversees and regulates wire and radio communications.

Follow-Up System   A procedure of providing the service required to complete a sale. The system may be manual or computerized.

FX (Foreign Exchange Lines)   Provides local telephone service from a central office that is outside or foreign to the subscriber.

Full Duplex   Communications systems or equipment that is capable of simultaneous transmission in two directions.

Group Paging   A feature of some telephone systems that allows for specified sets of extensions to be paged, such as sales, service, customer service, engineering, etc.

Headset   An apparatus composed of a microphone and a speaker(s) that fits on TSRs' heads or rests on an ear, permitting them to take calls hands-free. Sometimes referred to as a headpiece.

Hertz   A unit of signal frequency equal to one cycle per second.

Hybrid System   A telephone system that combines the attributes of more than one system.

In-Band   An ISDN term used with ANI (automatic number identification) or caller ID.

Inbound   All calls coming into a telemarketing center. Opposite of outbound.

In-House Telemarketing   Telemarketing done within a company as a primary or supplementary method of marketing and selling that company's products.

Interconnect Companies   These provide telephone equipment but not service.

Key System   Phone system characterized by buttons or keys that are pressed to access each line.

Least-Cost Routing (LCR)   Equipment that automatically selects the most economical method of placing a call.

Line   The transmission wire within a telephone system.

Line Capacity   The total number of in-house telephones a switch can handle.

Local Access and Transport Area (LATA)   The geographic regions served by the Bell Operating Companies Intra-LATA (local) telephone rates which are regulated, while Inter-LATA (long-distance) rates are deregulated.

Lookup Service   An organization that locates phone numbers for a fee.

Merge-Purge   The process of combining multiple lists into a single one and eliminating duplicates.

Modem A device that converts computer-generated digital signals into analog (voice) signals, which can be transported over telephone lines.

Monaural A headset built with one receiver so that sound is heard in only one ear.

Monitoring The ability to listen in on conversations on other extensions, usually for training purposes.

Multiplexer Allows one telephone line to be shared by several terminals.

Network A communications system connecting many devices, such as computers, printer, telephones, etc.

Night Service The mode in which a telephone system functions when unattended by a central or PBX operator.

Noise Canceling A feature of some headsets that reduces the amount of noise picked up by the microphone.

Off-Net Usually refers to geographic areas not accommodated by a long-distance carrier.

Open-Ended Probes Questions requiring something more than a simple yes or no answer. Similar to essay questions on a written questionnaire. Used to elicit broad, general information.

Outbound Call originating from a telemarketing call center. The opposite of inbound.

Page or Paging Attempting to locate someone by calling their name over a speaker system.

Park A feature on telephone systems, similar to hold, which keeps a call at an extension until it can be picked up by the proper person.

PBX Private Branch Exchanges (sometimes referred to as Private Automatic Branch Exchanges [PABX]). They are telephone switches that route calls to the extensions within organizations or businesses.

Phonathon A fundraising event conducted primarily via telephone.

Pre-call Planning Refers to the preparation TSRs do prior to commencing a calling session. A Pre-call Planning Checklist is included in Appendix 2.

Predictive Dialer Automatic dialing equipment using pacing algorithms to determine the rate at which outbound calls should be placed to assure that TSRs have an even supply of prospects to talk with. Discussed in Chapter 6.

Prospect A potential customer.

Protocol The established format for sending and receiving messages.

Pulse Code Modulation (PCM) The most commonly used method of converting analog signals into digital bits.

Pulse-Only Telephone A rotary phone.

Queuing Holds calls in order until they can be answered one at a time.

Redial A feature of telephone systems that permits TSRs to dial a number a second time with one keystroke. Often restricted to the last number dialed.

Reference Guide All the information TSRs need to conduct professional telemarketing efforts.

Remote Call Forwarding Allows calls to be sent to a remotely located telephone outside the system on which the call was received.

Roll-Out Major campaign following a test.

Routing Assigning a communications path to a telephone call so it will reach the desired destination.

RS-232-C The most common interface between computers and modems.

Script A prepared presentation to be used by TSRs.

SIC (Standard Industrial Classification) A classification of business used by U.S. Department of Commerce.

Smile'n'Dial A type of telemarketing in which TSRs call as many prospects as possible and deliver their message as quickly as possible. Opposite of consultative selling.

Speed Dialing See automatic dialing.

Station Detail Record A record of the calling activity of a station, extension, or TSR which usually includes number of calls made/attempted, call duration, trunk group utilized, and other useful information for managing a call center.

T-1 A trunk line of a digital telephone system for inbound and outbound long distance. Contains 24 channels or lines.

Telco A telephone operating company.

Telecollection Use of telemarketing skills to collect debts.

Telecommunications The transmission of audio information over a distance via electromagnetic means.

Telemarketing The planned use of the telephone in the marketing of products and services.

Telemedia   Combined use of the telephone with other media, such as fax machines and computers, to market products.

Teleresearcher   One trained to do research via the telephone.

Tie Lines   Two-way transmission voice circuits that directly connect PBXs or LANs.

Trunk   A communications channel linking a central office with a PBX or other type of terminal. It is the local line.

Trunk Capacity   The number of outgoing circuits.

TSR (Telemarketing Sales Representative)   An individual trained to communicate with customers and prospects over the phone. Also can mean telemarketing service rep or call center representative.

Turnkey System   A complete and fully assembled telephone system, including hardware and software. Most even include training of personnel.

Voice Response   Computer technology in which a caller "talks" with a computer via a telephone. In most cases, the caller responds to questions asked by the computer by touching keys on a digital telephone set.

Voice Technology   An all-inclusive term for electronic voice mail, interactive voice response (IRV), and voice recognition technology. All three facilitate the communications between humans with a computer as the intermediary.

WATS (Wide Area Telecommunication Service)   A discounted long-distance service.

Index